Psychoanalytic Theory of Art

A Philosophy of Art on
Developmental Principles

Psychoanalytic Theory of Art

A Philosophy of Art on Developmental Principles

RICHARD KUHNS

COLUMBIA UNIVERSITY PRESS
NEW YORK   1983

Library of Congress Cataloging in Publication Data

Kuhns, Richard Francis, 1924–
  Psychoanalytic theory of art.

  Bibliography: p.
  Includes index.
  1. Psychoanalysis and art. 2. Art—Philosophy.
I. Title.
N72.P74K8 1983   701   82-23499
ISBN 0-231-05620-6
ISBN 0-231-05621-4 (pbk.)

Columbia University Press
New York   Guildford, Surrey

10 9 8 7 6 5 4 3 2

Contents

Preface

Beginning with Freud's earliest writings it was recognized that psychoanalytic thought contained and expressed, though incompletely, a philosophy of art. Building upon that early affinity of the theory for works of art, the following inquiry presents a philosophy of art on developmental principles, the principles that gave structure to the theory from its first experimentations through to its contemporary and growing body of thought and application. I shall argue that, in a sense larger than any understood by Freud and his close followers, psychoanalytic theory can be usefully elaborated into a philosophy of art. As a philosophy of art, the psychoanalytic theory of art stands in a position to put forward a critique of several basic assumptions which in the past have been major supports to the philosophies of art in the Western tradition. It is in its two capacities as explanatory theory, and as a well-grounded critique of modern philosophy of art, that the following chapters present psychoanalytic thought.

My presentation has two dominant themes that it follows throughout the argument: one has to do with *interpretation*, the method whereby psychoanalytic theory comes to its findings about art and artists, persons and culture; and the other has to do with the *objects* themselves that the theory attempts to interpret. I call the objects in their generic being "enactments," by which I mean to include a large variety of objects that fill our lives as cultural beings, and out of that large domain I shall select for interpretation linguistic and material objects we refer to, most casually, as "art." Although Freud thought a good bit about cultural objects and their importance to the cultural side of human action, his own writing contains but a few essays devoted to culture as such; however, they are of deep importance and are a part of the foundation upon which my elaboration can rest. Yet that foundation remained unconnected to the theory of objects during Freud's career, and the two sides of the theory—the speculations on culture, and the clinical observations and interpretations of art objects—were united and elaborated only by those followers of Freud working in England and the United States.

My interest, because it is more philosophical than that of many other theorists, leads me to follow out the implications of the psychoanalytic theory of culture in the direction of a philosophy of art. It is my contention that philosophy today in the Anglo-American tradition stands in need of many of the ideas that psychoanalytic theory proposes, and that for our purposes where a philosophy of art is concerned, the most fruitful approach is *developmental*. Therefore the analysis in the following chapters assumes that a maturational as well as a historical sequence informs the cultural function of art. The developmental enables a philosophy of art to realize, as well, deeply important aspects of the individual capacity to make, use, and respond to art. The developmental, as I use the concept, has two dimensions: in the growth of the person, and in the history of each art. Because my approach to the philosophy of art is through a theory of *enactments*, and because I emphasize the importance of history to the developmental treatment of objects, I regard the physical medium of cultural objects to be an essential focus for a psychoanalytic theory of art. I therefore classify the arts in terms of their media, as material (painting, sculpture, architecture, the dance in part), tonal (music, vocalization, the dance in part), and linguistic (both written and oral narration).

Stages in the history of the arts, as they are mastered by artists, and stages in an individual artist's life, are functions of one another; and although it is the task of art history to map these interrelationships, it is the task of a philosophy of art to give theoretical justification for such affinities. Of course, the process of an individual's maturation occurs in history, and the tendency of psychoanalytic theory to ignore history must be dealt with as a limitation, yet one that can be overcome. In speaking of development and maturation, I do not imply that the later is better. It is assumed, however, that in both persons and in history the later is developmentally related to what has gone before. It should be noted that a developmental view in the psychological sense is not characteristic of modern philosophy.

The story I tell here is essentially of persons and cultural objects in their psychological development. Their developmental interrelationships occur in large part through the process we have come to call "interpretation," the agency for the determination of meaning, properties, and implications. It is also, in its historical use, a way to discover the elements and causal complexities of a *tradition*. For persons and objects do not inhabit an atomistic universe, but rather share a cultural universe whose structure and direction can be discovered through interpretation. When that reality is clearly established—a realization pursued by generations—a tradition becomes known. The search for the tradition, and the mastery of objects is the work of culture: *culture is a tradition of enactments*.

The inquiry begins with a brief statement of the affinity between psychoanalytic theory of art and its philosophical antecedents. I shall argue that Freud's way of thinking about and interpreting art has its roots in the positivistic and idealistic theories of the nineteenth century, especially Hegel's philosophy of art. However, it will be clear that in certain respects

Freud's interest in culture is quite different from the philosophical interpretations of idealism.

To prepare the way for a psychoanalytic theory of culture—beyond the limitations Freud set for his own speculations—the second chapter will follow the discussion of philosophical affinities with a compressed and selective discussion of the concepts basic to the theory in all its applications. I do not give detailed expositions of psychoanalytic thought, assuming some familiarity with it, and access to the complete mapping of the theory is provided by books listed in the bibliography.

The third chapter will set forth a psychoanalytic theory of culture, applying to *Totem and Taboo,* and to *Moses and Monotheism* interpretative methods that are common to philosophic modes of analysis: I shall consider Freud's writings on culture as if they were in some measure philosophic in their vision and method, which indeed they are, though to what degree Freud recognized this I cannot say. As the theory unfolds into a philosophy of art, use will be made of English and American contributions to a more fully developed theory of cultural objects, beyond Freud's own thought.

The fourth chapter, with its demonstrations of how psychoanalytic theory works when addressed to art, will point out some of the difficulties the theory has encountered, and ways to overcome the difficulties by making use of the conceptual restructuring introduced in chapter 3.

The final chapter will consider ways in which psychoanalytic theory and art history contribute to and reinforce one another. To make the complementarity sharp and constructive, this chapter, like the one before, will present interpretations to illustrate the theory in the form that, in my view, endows it with explanatory power.

Together, the five chapters are brief and illustrative for a subject of such complexity; my purpose is to provide what I hope to be a useful accompaniment to the work of art history, literary criticism, and philosophical anthropology. Psychoanalytic theory of art, in its philosophical implications, should, it seems to me, be readily available in a short exposition from which inquiry can then move on to consult longer, more detailed, and more specialized studies.

The whole exposition, it will be seen, keeps close to Freud's clinical work and theory, for it is my belief that a psychoanalytic theory of art must ground itself in psychoanalytic thought at its clearest and most powerful. And in that respect I find today a neglect of more basic conceptualization for a kind of freewheeling thematic variation. Where contemporary theory does build upon Freud's thought in a systematic way, I shall refer to it, and chapter 3 draws upon recent ego psychology and object relations theory to develop the concept of the object necessary to a philosophy of art. Many recent schools and theories have, obviously, simply been ignored; while I recognize the importance of their contributions, the developmental philosophy of art offered here is essentially "Freudian" in the sense that it sets itself in a tradition guided by the texts Freud wrote. Because of the pervasive philosophical influences upon these writings, Freud's theory often speaks directly to the needs of the philosophy of art, and it is in that strong, well-known tradition that I write.

In giving an exposition of psychoanalytic theory of art, and in attempting to expand it beyond its own conscious boundaries, I bring to a close a set of like expositions devoted to those thinkers whose contributions to the philosophy of art have been, in my opinion, revolutionary.

Acknowledgments

I wish to thank the following friends and colleagues for their stimulation, criticism, and support throughout the writing of this book: Robert Austerlitz, Helen Bacon, Bernard Beckerman, Robert Belknap, Arthur Collins, Linda Collins, Robert Cumming, Arthur Danto, Stanley Eveling, Ruth Gay, Martin Greenberg, Howard Hibbard, Norman Holland, David Hoy, Robert Liebert, David Sidorsky. I owe a special debt of gratitude to Peter Gay, Dieter Henrich, and Eric Marcus, who read and made comments on the work in progress. I have tried to incorporate their suggestions and creative criticism. In addition, I am grateful to Dieter Henrich for suggesting that I write an essay on the psychoanalytic theory of art which formed the kernel of this book. Above all, I want to thank my wife, Margaret Kuhns, for her constant support and encouragement, and for the many discussions we have had on the issues in this book.

I wish to thank Otto Kernberg for his permission to quote from an unpublished paper presented to the symposium, Modern Concepts of the Unconscious.

A large part of the research for this book was supported by a grant from the National Endowment for the Humanities.

Psychoanalytic Theory of Art

A Philosophy of Art on
Developmental Principles

In the summer vacation of the year 189-, I made an excursion into the Hohe Tauern so that for a while I might forget medicine and more particularly the neuroses. I had almost succeeded in this when one day I turned aside from the main road to climb a mountain which lay somewhat apart and which was renowned for its views and for its well-run refuge hut. I reached the top after a strenuous climb and, feeling refreshed and rested, was sitting deep in contemplation of the charm of the distant prospect. I was so lost in thought that at first I did not connect it with myself when these words reached my ears: 'Are you a doctor, sir?' But the question was addressed to me, and by the rather sulky-looking girl of perhaps eighteen who had served my meal and had been spoken to by the landlady as 'Katarina.' To judge by her dress and bearing, she could not be a servant, but must no doubt be a daughter or relative of the landlady's.

Coming to myself I replied: 'Yes, I'm a doctor: but how did you know that?'

'You wrote your name in the Visitor's Book, sir. And I thought if you had a few moments to spare. . . . The truth is, sir, my nerves are bad. I went to see a doctor in L_____ about them and he gave me something for them; but I'm not well yet.'

So there I was with the neuroses once again—for nothing else could very well be the matter with this strong, well-built girl with her happy look. I was interested to find that neuroses could flourish in this way at a height of over 6,000 feet; I questioned her further therefore. I report the conversation that followed between us just as it is impressed on my memory and I have not altered the patient's dialect.

—*Studies on Hysteria* (Std. Ed., 2:125)

I

Introduction: The Place of Psychoanalytic Theory in Philosophy of Art

The art of every cultural tradition presupposes a theory of art, and without a knowledge of the theory, the art itself remains insufficiently understood and enjoyed. In some traditions—for example, in that we refer to as "primitive art"—the theory is unwritten, yet still articulable, and the possession of a recognized keeper of the theory. In other traditions, such as our own recent architectural programs, theory parades itself as a necessary part of the built objects; and in contemporary painting of the West theory has changed with every style and school. Though theory today insinuates itself into the created thing, the importance and influence of theory upon art from ancient Greece to our own time is clearly established. Often art found its theory in statements produced by philosophers, and in this tradition there are many philosophies of art to yield up theory, though few philosophies of art that can be called "revolutionary." By "revolutionary theory" I mean those few that have deeply altered the way art is produced, used, and understood. It is correct, I believe, to propose the view that to understand the art of the West, one must be acquainted with the thought of the few revolutionary thinkers who devoted serious thought to art, and contributed the theory which lives within and around the arts themselves.

I consider the following to make up the select company of revolutionary theorists: Plato, Aristotle, St. Augustine, Kant, Hegel, Freud. To conclude the list with a clinical doctor and psychoanalytic psychiatrist may seem odd, but there is no doubt that Freud's theory of psychic life, and his method of interpreting psychological events has had a profound—indeed a revolutionary—effect upon the creation, use, and appreciation of works of art, not only those produced since Freud wrote but also the works of the past which have been reconsidered in the light of his theory.

Whenever a revolutionary theory of art appears, it has the effect of compelling us to reconsider the whole tradition to which it contributes a part; think of the theoretical and practical changes that have occurred as a consequence of Hegel's philosophy of art. Because of Hegel we see the whole history of art in a new way; indeed, in a fundamental respect there was no history of art as we understand it until Hegel. So, too, the thought of St. Augustine worked a radical deformation upon the traditional critical stance taken toward classical art. Augustine's extensive commentaries upon texts, his methodological treatises, such as the *De Doctrina Christiana,* revealed the power of art as symbolic expression and gave us the techniques to enlarge and to deepen modes of expression in art. Because of Augustine's philosophy of language, of symbol, and of music, the art of his own time, as well as the art that succeeded him, was given a coherent and consistent interpretation.

Such theoretical renovations following from a theory mark the history of art and the philosophy of art in the West. Usually, a philosophy of art grows out of a general philosophical exploration that must include problems in the theory of knowledge and in ontology. In contrast, Freud's theory of art developed from a number of different explorations. First of all, it grew out of his discovery that important works of art had dealt with the deep psychological problems he encountered as part of his clinical work. Further, Freud had an interest in language, especially its use in poetry and literature, and in the symbolic content of visual art. But there is another source to his theory of art, and that is his own natural narrative gifts, for a distinguishing characteristic of Freud's writing is its story-like structure. From the earliest case studies published in a collection alongside studies by Breuer, to his last writing on the Biblical Moses, Freud wrote "stories," adventures of persons in their psychological travails and quests. If the case studies themselves are taken as documents, with no concern for their literary quality, they give a full and penetrating presentation of the lives, characters, and social organizations of the European middle class at the turn of the century. In addition, the narratives often have the suspense and moral impact of great literature.[1]

We might consider Freud's writing an exploration and elaboration of a late-nineteenth century genre, the clinical narrative. Introduced to that mode of narration through his collaboration with Josef Breuer, Freud took hold of it and developed it into a complex literary form in which plot alternates with theory, theory with character analysis, and the events taking place in the consulting room are shown to have their towardness in the larger conflicts of communal life. If we set Freud's writing in the clinic where it originated, it accords in many ways with other cultural products of its time. There is, to use Mannheim's phrase, "a documentary meaning" in the case histories that portrays a *Weltanschauung*. Although Freud denied that psychoanalysis expressed its own *Weltanschauung*, we see aspects of his work in coherence with other activities of his time, and those continuities and affinities will be of help in developing psychoanalytic theory as a philosophy of art.[2] To a great extent, of course, Freud was conscious of the affinities between the arts and clinical practice; he drew upon contemporary literary art and various arts of the past for examples to support his own findings. His deep interest in and eagerness to exploit the arts on behalf of his theory are demonstrated by the essays he wrote on works of art and on artists.

One of the reasons for Freud's preoccupation with artists and art works was his recognition of their psychological acuity; the artists knew, somehow, a great deal of what Freud was trying to find out; they anticipated him, and yet they were not fully aware of the riches of their own thought. To make explicit and theoretically defensible many of the insights of writers and painters was a purpose Freud early conceived and expressed in his letters to Wilhelm Fliess, to whom he wrote that in the drama *Hamlet* were many of the insights he struggled to clarify.[3] His discovery, for so he termed it, of the "secret of *Hamlet*" led him to affirm the psychoanalytic penetration of much art, and to use artistic discoveries to support some of his own. In this respect, Freud's theory of art is as closely tied to actual works of art as is that of Plato or that of Hegel.

Curiously, however, Freud remained content with a relatively impoverished exploitation of his theory in its capacity as a theory of art. He had his favorite themes and characters, and artistic geniuses to whom he turned again and again for examples. But outside of a few essays, many scattered references to art, a brief discussion of folktales, fairy tales, and a popular novel of his day (Jensen's *Gradiva*), Freud never made extended and consistent use of his theory in the analysis of art, and much of his theory which would have been most helpful in developing a philosophy of art was never put to that use.

So there is a lack where we would expect a superabundance of discussion, and even subsequent psychoanalytic writers on art have not taken hold of all that is useful in Freud's theory. Therefore, to understand what would constitute a psychoanalytic theory of art, we face problems that do not beset us in the explication of other philosophical systems. There is first, Freud's negelect of some of his own thoughts in their relevance to art; second, the incomplete and unsatisfactory development of some of Freud's ideas in writings by other philosophers and psychoanalysts; and, third, the lack of a systematic exposition of an explicit psychoanalytic theory of art. In this essay I shall try to develop a psychoanalytic theory of art that will overcome these deficiencies.

In explicating a psychoanalytic theory of art, the historical location of Freud's thoughts about art should be recognized. Although psychoanalytic concepts have their origin in physical, evolutionary, physiological, and chemical theories of the nineteenth century, Freud's views on art can be classified as *philosophic* in a specific sense: Freud's views on art are consistent with, and may even be partially derived from, the idealistic philosophy of Hegel. This is not to argue that Freud read Hegel, or had any interest in Hegel as a thinker, although in the university Freud undoubtedly had opportunities to hear lectures that shared in an idealistic view of history, art, and culture. In Freud's student years, Hegel's philosophy was no longer the powerful force it had been in the early years of the nineteenth century, yet there was a legacy of expressionistic theories of art to which Freud could readily attach his own interests in the developmental vicissitudes of human consciousness. For all his avowed dissociation from philosophic thought, Freud nevertheless put forward a mode of expressionist philosophy of art which is in several respects like that presented in Hegel's posthumously published lectures known as the *Ästhetik*.[4] In the *Ästhetik* Hegel argues that art works "express" ideas and that the ideas can be understood in terms of both a historical and a conceptual progress as achieving every-increasing ranges of self-consciousness. When works of art are interpreted according to Hegel's method (which is really his philosophy as a system), they yield cultural points of view, or *Weltanschauungen*. It is the philosopher's task to see these partial aspects of mind in their totality as part of a larger cultural history. Philosophy in fact constitutes that method by means of which this continual interpretation is carried out. Hegel called his method a science (*Wissenschaft*); he saw its intellectual goal as the complete working out of the ever-changing and evolving aspects of consciousness, which his philosophical vision described as but a part of the larger evolution of spirit (*Geist*). The evolution, he argued, is thoroughly historical, so that his method can accommodate art history as we know it, but it is art history of a complex sort whose ultimate unfolding and explication is never done.

Despite his fascination with the grander vistas of spirit, Hegel is above all the historian of consciousness and its interpretations; Freud is the psychologist of unconsciousness, and the paths the unconscious takes to consciousness. Hegel locates the art he analyzes in an ideal historical typology, classifying all of cultural objects as Symbolic, or Classical, or Romantic; Freud is not concerned with the historical location of art, since the themes psychoanalysis deals with are ever-present, recurring motifs that appear in the earliest art we know, and continue in one guise or another down to our own time. In opposition to a presumed timelessness of artistic themes, Hegel would have argued for a conception of art as a growing, evolving, ever-more-inclusive product, to be succeeded by a yet fuller, more adequate expression of consciousness. To Hegel's art history Arnold Hauser has given the title "art history without names"; to Freud's theory of art we might attach the title "names without history," for art and artists express their internal conflicts, and these remain constant in all historical periods.

Although Freud would agree with Hegel that cultural products require interpretation, the inner or true meaning of an event is stated by different sets of categories and different formulations to explain the sources and means of resolving conflict within the two theories, as we shall see in the chapters to follow. However, there are areas the two theories do agree upon, both in the conception of what it is to establish an interpretation, and the means whereby we can identify clarified consciousness. On those grounds I would suggest that psychoanalytic theory of art is both historically and methodologically in the tradition of idealistic expressionism, and I shall explore the affinity in the examples offered below.

Freud's conception of cultural conflict centers on a ubiquitous set of inevitable psychosexual problems and on the drive of aggression; Hegel's conception dwells upon moral, political, epistemological, and ontological positions constantly evolving because of a force, a dialectical process and a resolution, which constitutes the history of human consciousness in its cultural expression. Time is a necessary condition for resolution of conflict in both theories; but for Hegel it is the time of vast sweeps of history; for Freud it is time in the maturational process from infancy to adulthood. Freud's theory of cultural products, like his theory of the person, is developmental in the psychological sense; Hegel's theory is developmental in a historical sense. Both theories use the idea of repression, although it is only by analogy from psychoanalysis to idealistic philosophy that repression can be recognized as a concept in Hegel's writing. In the person, and in history, feelings, beliefs, thoughts, expectations, dreams, and fantasies are repressed. That is to say, interpretation, when exercised upon human products, discovers an unconscious domain which is a necessary condition for, and an inevitable accompaniment of, a conscious domain. The forces responsible for repression are measured and described in each theory.

Each theory copes with repression differently: for Hegel, philosophical analysis lays bare and brings to consciousness ideas, beliefs, attitudes, and world perspectives that the participants in cultures now gone could not have recognized. The history of philosophy is in part the activity of interpretation, bringing past repressions into present consciousness. For Freud, whose preoccupations were clinical and therapeutic, repression refers to individual unconscious aspects of psychic life. The emphasis in psychoanalytic theory is upon conflict which prevents unconscious material from reaching consciousness, and sees repression therefore as a vicissitude of the instinctual side of human psychic life. Repression is a force within the self that turns an idea away from consciousness. And that force, operating in artists, is represented and expressed in art, as it also works in the perceivers of art shaping their conscious responses. A task of psychoanalytic theory when it takes up interpretation is parallel to that of Hegelian idealism, but directed to the individual in the psychosexual conflicts which characterize growing up in culture. Therefore psychoanalytic theory of art recognizes the force and success of repression in every aspect of art-making and use. As we shall see, a psychoanalytic interpretation of an artist, of a work of art, and of the critical response to a work of art, tells a story in basic respects different from the Hegelian story. That does not mean, however, that the two tellings are at odds with each other, or irreconcilable. They often will complement each other in ways that help us to understand and to respond deeply to works of art.

In pointing out the likenesses and differences between Hegelian and Freudian approaches to art, I want to emphasize the philosophical implications of the comparison: Freud's psychoanalytic variation of a fundamental idealistic way to understand culture and cultural products is one of several possible and actualized variations that have made nineteenth and twentieth-century philosophy of art the richest in a long tradition. Indeed, there is a remarkable prescience in Hegel's anticipations of art forms and art theories that he suspected would fill the minds of artists and philosophers. There are passages in Hegel's *Ästhetik* in which he describes the increasing narcissism of the modern artist, and an artistic preoccupation with inwardness to which psychoanalytic theory, we may now realize, was a fitting and appropriate correlate.[5]

It should be remembered that there are other versions of expression theory following Schelling and Hegel: Marx, Nietzsche, Husserl, Heidegger, Collingwood, Sartre are all indebted to Hegel in their reflections on art; each of their positions explores different ways in which expression theory can be developed. In this respect psychoanalytic theory belongs to a group of theories, and stands firmly in the intellectual climate that gave distinction to Western thought in the nineteenth and early twentieth centures. The expressionist revolution in art theory followed from developments in the arts themselves, and made a substantial contribution to the ways the arts were shaped, interpreted, and responded to. Although the psychoanalytic theory of art has sometimes been denigrated by its philosophical critics as aberrant, it really participated in and made an original contribution to a movement in nineteenth- and twentieth-century thought whose implications we are continuing to discover and to exploit. Our avidity for collection, our passion for critical interpretation, our scholarly commitment to the history of art and culture call upon idealistic theories of art in all their power and diversity.

Despite these preoccupations of our time, the affinities of psychoanalytic theory of art to the idealistic theories established by Schelling and Hegel have not been noted by contemporary followers of Freud. The strong philosophical tendencies in Freud's thought do not, as a rule, dominate post-Freudian speculations on art. There is no reason why they should be as philosophically ambitious as was Freud's speculation; but the diminution in philosophical striving has affected recent inquiry; recent contributions tend toward strict psychological interpretation of painting and literature. There is, I believe, a need to continue to push out the philosophical frontier in Freud's work because that will open the way for more original and more varied psychoanalytic interpretations. The tradition has had a tendency to become repetitive and routine. One of the purposes, then, of this study is to enlarge the philosophical themes—sometimes latent—in Freud's own thought, and to search out contributions, by both philosophers and psychoanalysts, that will help psychoanalytic theory realize all of which it is capable.

There is a wide range of writings on art and theory that will be helpful in this effort. As the following chapters develop, they will include more and more of the work that follows upon Freud's original investigations. Some of the contributions will be from art historians and literary critics, some from philosophers, and many from psychoanalytic theories attempting to extend the power and scope of psychoanalysis as an account of human psychic life. However, the interest I have is more in theory than in the many applications that have been made to individual works of art and artists. While I contribute some of my own interpretative work, I will reserve the bibliography for most of the interpretative contributions, hoping in this way to direct the reader to studies on individual lives, periods, and problems.

When we look for the most promising recent theoretical contributions to psychoanalytic theory, we find a great deal that has to do with revision of our understanding of ego psychology and infant development. Much of this is clinically specific and difficult to generalize toward a philosophy of art. I believe, however, that some of the basic theoretical contributions of Anna Freud, Melanie Klein, Heinz Hartmann, D. W. Winnicott, Kurt Eissler, Edith Jacobson, Margaret Mahler, Otto Kernberg, and others are relevant to the enlargement of theory that I hope to achieve, and where it seems to me their ideas make a contribution I will discuss them.

II

The Structure of the Theory
for a Philosophy of Art

European philosophy was the larger background for the development of psychoanalytic theory; the more immediate and imminent influences flowed from the natural sciences and medicine. The deepest, most pervasive force upon Freud's thought was the Newtonian vision of the universe generated and sustained by a belief in a hidden reality beyond the sensory capacity of humans but available ultimately through the inferential powers of mathematics and the laws of natural science. Psychoanalytic theory shared the Newtonian *Weltanschauung* and, drawn by Freud's vision of psychic life, set upon a quest for the secret inner of experience, analogous to that outer sought by physics in the natural order. Newton and Freud bracketed human experience as a domain between two unknowables, a phenomenal realm of limited sense awareness and a limited inner awareness, whose confinement sentences humankind to the hard labor of discovering, by various inferential methods, the realities without and within. Freud regarded his quest for the revelation of inner reality as one that had already been undertaken, successfully in regard to nature, by the natural scientists in the tradition to which he gave his allegiance.

But the medical science Freud sought to establish had to move in a direction just the opposite of Newtonian physics which could readily accept the distinction between perceptual immediacy and the construction of hidden outer reality through theory. Psychoanalytic theory was addressed to uncovering an *inner* psychic reality through a distinction between conscious and unconscious. The psychoanalytic quest for an unrecognized and heretofore unknown inner reality sought what had escaped the investigations of both the natural scientists and the philosophers. Freud pointed out, with considerable self-satisfaction, that his conclusions completed a scientific organization of nature and human psychic life that the enlightenment and nineteenth-century positivism failed to complete.

Psychoanalytic theory was developed with both the philosophical and the scientific thinking of the modern tradition as models; but modern philosophy, Freud believed, though it had succeeded in its application of Newtonian dualism to nature, had failed in its exploration of the mind. And it was to be the signal achievement of psychoanalytic theory that it would complete what philosophy had been unable to realize. The method of modern philosophy, which distinguished percept from object, was, in Freud's view, the counterpart to the need to distinguish conscious psychic life from unconscious psychic life. Consistency in the recognition of a necessary dualism would result in a thoroughgoing scientific foundation for the medical analysis of psychic life. Freud's self-consciousness in drawing the parallel between psychoanalysis and the physical sciences, and his insistence that psychoanalysis completed the incompleteness of philosophy, provide us with an understanding of how he regarded and valued his own discoveries. It is in the light of his method that he then went on to interpret cultural objects, such as works of art.

I In *The Interpretation of Dreams* Freud argued that the process of dream interpretation has led to an understanding of mental life with a thoroughness and a theoretical adequacy that philosophy, with its traditional concern for consciousness, has not yielded. Sharp criticism is directed against theories of consciousness proposed in Hegelian and post-Hegelian idealism;

and although Freud is never explicit about whom he is attacking, he makes it clear that he regards psychoanalytic theory as in competition with philosophy.

These considerations may lead us to feel that the interpretation of dreams may enable us to draw conclusions as to the structure of our mental apparatus which we have hoped for in vain from philosophy.[1]

Late in the book he writes:

So long as psychology dealt with this problem by a verbal explanation to the effect that 'psychical' *meant* 'conscious' and that to speak of 'unconscious psychical processes' was palpable nonsense, any psychological evaluation of the observations made by physicians upon abnormal mental states was out of the question. The physician and the philosopher can only come together if they both recognize that the term 'unconscious psychical processes' is the appropriate and justified expression of a solidly established fact.[2]

Freud's contention is that in posing the question "what is the nature of consciousness?" philosophy has never looked to clinical medicine for an answer. And, therefore, philosophy has never realized that in the medical treatment of mental life, the physician commonly "feel[s] at liberty to proceed by *inference* from the conscious effect to the unconscious psychical process," and then can draw the conclusion that "the conscious effect is only a remote physical result of the unconscious process . . . and that the latter was present and operative even without betraying its existence in any way to consciousness."[3] Philosophy, mistakenly, has always developed its arguments from the observations of thought as it is *consciously* entertained by the philosopher in the process of thinking. The isolated position of the philosopher makes it difficult, if not dangerous, to consider psychic life as Freud came to understand it while working with his patients. From this work, Freud concluded, in a passage that asserts his essential critique of philosophy, that the

unconscious is the larger sphere, which includes within it the smaller sphere of the conscious. Everything conscious has an unconscious preliminary stage; whereas what is unconsciousness may remain at that stage and nevertheless claim to be regarded as having the full value of a psychical process. The unconsciousness is the true psychical reality; *in its innermost nature it is as much unknown to us as the reality of the external world, and it is as incompletely presented by the data of consciousness as is the external world by the communication of the sense organs.*[4]

I quote these passages at length because the views stated are basic to all of Freud's thought, and because these views pose the psychoanalytic challenge to the assumptions of philosophic thought as Freud knew them. Freud created, partly as a reaction against certain idealistic philosophical views, partly as a critique of certain empiricistic epistemological views, an epistemology that derives an inner unknown as a parallel to the outer unknown of philosophical tradition. It is this challenge to traditional epistemology and to the assumption of the clarity and self-evidence of consciousness that provides the framework for Freud's analysis of psychological events, among which he came to include works of art. The nineteenth-century psychoanalyst conducted a search for inner reality with the same intensity as the eighteenth-century philosopher conducted a quest for external reality.

The exploration of inner psychological reality inevitably raised the question, Why is there a hidden inner reality that is so difficult to lay bare? Unlike the inaccessibility of external physical reality, psychological reality seemed to be heavily defended and kept inaccessible by the wish of the person. Discovery did not rely simply on better "machines" and more sophisticated "science" as in physics, but rather on breaking through willful, though unconscious, defenses. The hidden psychological was in some sense—at first difficult to understand—dangerous, or unconsciously perceived as threatening. Hence getting through to it required a method that would prove to be highly original and experimentally variable, suited to the individual who came to the clinic. At the same time that Freud was working out his clinical procedures, he observed the occurrence of hidden psychic reality in cultural products that were available to all. In some ways, perhaps in ways not unlike the defenses of his patients, cultural events, like novels and paintings, were able at once to present and keep obscure the very things that in private action led to neurosis and psychosis.

In the effort to understand the forces responsible for repression, and to clarify the content of the unconscious, Freud came to realize that the search for psychological reality required a double attack. On the one side unconscious processes themselves had to be discovered and their dynamic described; on the other, the products of unconscious process had to be studied. The most available and the most interesting products of unconscious psychological reality are dreams.

Freud faced the task of determining what is "really" going on in dreaming, and he reached conclusions that are still surprising, even though his views have been so thoroughly reconsidered over the last sixty years.

At bottom, dreams are nothing other than a particular *form* of thinking, made possible by the conditions of the state of sleep. It is the *dream-work* which creates the form, and it alone is the essence of dreaming—the explanation of its peculiar nature. . . . The fact that dreams concern themselves with attempts at solving the problems by which our mental life is faced is no more strange than that our conscious waking life should do so; beyond this it merely tells us that that activity can also be carried on in the preconscious—and this we already knew.[5]

Contrary to earlier assumptions about the disorder and irrationality of dreams and of the unconscious, there is in dreams a structure and an interpretable set of symbols which, though not linguistic in all cases, can nevertheless be given a meaning.

The dream-thoughts are entirely rational and are constructed with an expenditure of all the psychical energy of which we are capable. They have their place among the thought-processes that have not become conscious—processes from which, after some modification, our conscious thoughts, too, arise.[6]

This is a fundamental observation on which the theory is erected, and appears again and again as a part of the apparatus used to interpret psychic products, such as works of art. The distinction between "thought processes that have not become conscious" and "conscious thought" provides the ground on which a crucial distinction between latent content and manifest content rests. This dualism is essential to Freud's explanation of psychic life, and I shall discuss it below.

Freud's dualism of manifest and latent implies a deep critique of philosophical assumptions, for it has been philosophically relevant to attempt a distinction between "appearance" and "reality," but always on the presupposition that one in some sense could "know" them both. Freud, in contrast, thinks of reality as enclosing, psychologically, an appearing and a real, even though he writes as if he sees the inferences to the unconscious as parallel to the inference philosophy makes from perception to an underlying reality. And he does not assume that psychological "reality" can be fully known. Although Freud presents his views as the obverse of a philosophical tradition, they are really conceptually far more revolutionary than he recognized. They enable him to distinguish the "dream-work"—that is, what we experience as the dream—from the "dream-thoughts"—that is, the dream in its unconscious aspect as a meaningful statement, when properly interpreted.

Although the phrase "the dream in its unconscious aspect" is puzzling to the philosophical tradition, we must always bear in mind that Freud investigates "psychic reality" which he conceives as possessing the structure of a large sphere within which a smaller sphere of consciousness identifies us to ourselves, and gives us the ground and starting point for the exploration of the larger unconscious reality. "Reality" includes both manifest and latent psychic events. When we make inferences from manifest to latent, we move from dream-work to dream-thoughts. The reversal of the philosophical terminology is important. Philosophers go from "thought" to that which lies inferentially beyond thought, while the psychoanalytic method moves from bits of conscious evidence *to thought*. Thus the psychoanalytic quest begins with evidential fragments and concludes with what one *really* believes and thinks. Although the dream-thoughts are rational and ultimately can be understood precisely, the dream-work is quite different:

The dream-work is not simply more careless, more irrational, more forgetful, more incomplete than waking thought; it is completely different from it qualitatively and for that reason not immediately comparable with it. It does not think, calculate, or judge in any way at all; it restricts itself to giving things a new form. . . . That product, the dream, has above all to evade the censorship, and with that end in view the dream-work makes use of displacement of psychical intensities to the point of a transvaluation of all psychical values.[7]

Thus dreams are to be interpreted, and ultimately understood, as statements through their manifest (i.e., given and remembered), and their latent (i.e., hidden and inferred) content. It is this distinction, as well as the distinction conscious-unconscious, that runs throughout the psychoanalytic interpretation of psychic life. The manifest content of a dream is conscious; the latent content is probably, but not necessarily, unconscious. It is certainly unconscious until brought into conscious focus, but the term "unconscious" has attached to it various degrees of accessibility. What is unconscious may be readily accessible in some instances, and inaccessible in other instances. But the variable availability of material not immediately in consciousness led Freud to postulate a structure between the conscious and the unconscious, the preconscious, whose content was believed to be recallable at will. Although the discriminations between conscious, preconscious, and unconscious made by Freud in his early discussions of the psychic processes is today often slighted, there is some justification for our purposes to mention the early conceptualization. The usefulness of the concept preconscious emerges when we analyze the process of interpretation as it occurs in the response to works of art. Some material is available only through elaborate reconstruction, and some appears readily, either because it is not threatening or—and this is the interesting case—because it participates in established structures internal to the artistic tradition. The experiences we have with art are surprising because they permit often unavailable thought to suddenly occupy our consciousness. It is as if works of art have the power to transport certain thoughts from the unconscious to the preconscious through their having been, as it were, "aestheticized." The whole complex activity of art-making and art-using can be understood as a cultural loosening of the ordinarily rigid boundaries of the unconscious and the conscious. However, in general, when psychoanalytic theory asserts that the content of a dream, a slip of the tongue, a work of art express unconscious material, it is assumed that the unconscious or latent content is not accessible without interpretation.

"Interpretation," a common term for a variety of means to understanding texts and cultural products in general, comes in the psychoanalytic application to take on a specific meaning. "Interpretation" refers to a method whereby unconscious material is brought into consciousness through the lifting of repression. (I shall discuss repression below, pp. 25–31.) Thus, psychological reality continues to be conceptualized in a way parallel to the nineteenth-century conceptualization of nature: reality, whether physical or psychological, is approached from two points of view and from the inquiring activities of two investigators with different interests. The physical sciences distinguished nature as perceived by the naïve, unaccommodated person simply acting on animal impulse and animal faith, from the sophisticated interpretation of reality made by the scientist, who penetrated beyond appearances to the way events *really are*. In the clinical setting, the two points of view and two interests are those of the patient and the therapist who together aim to penetrate appearances—i.e., conscious psychic processes—to uncover and to understand unconscious psychic processes. Interpretation in the clinical setting implies bringing unconscious material to conscious awareness, and integrating the two so that continuities, contradictions, "meanings" in the broadest sense can emerge. Following out the parallel to scientific inquiry, the patient begins as the naïve observer, and presumably will end as the sophisticated knower. But along the way to that sought outcome there are stages of awareness and integration that we must consider in order to bring psychoanalytic theory to its full bearing upon the interpretation of works of art.

II The relationship between therapist and patient, with which psychoanalytic theory begins, and out of which it grew to encompass a great variety of relationships, objects, and things, expresses differences in the interpretation of events through the different points of view of the therapist and patient. There is a continuity to be recognized and traced from clinical analysis to cultural interpretation, for differences in points of view in the clinical setting are to be found as well in the psychoanalytic study of cultural objects. The different perspectives of therapist and patient have been characterized by the term "transference," and I shall extend the concept beyond the clinical situation to the interpretation of cultural objects.

Freud's use of the term "transference" was much more limited than the use it has assumed in subsequent psychoanalytic theory. For Freud, "transference," (*Übertragung*) referred to something that happens in the therapeutic exchange between patient and analyst: a reliving and repossessing of stages of development that had been gone through at earlier times in the psychosexual developmental process. The therapeutic use of transference was to interpret the earlier stages, integrate and understand them, and therefore achieve cure through their being now part of the conscious ego-controlled content of psychic life. To achieve that degree of awareness, the patient and therapist had to play out a complex interrelationship in which the therapist was endowed with many of the powers, attributes, wishes, and characteristics of the figures who had appeared in the patient's past. In short, the therapeutic situation reproduced and represented many of the earlier stages and specific events of the patient's psychological history. And, to that extent, every clinical situation would be unique.

Contemporary uses of the concept are broader, and therapeutically more refined, than those alluded to above. Now "transference" includes all that has been indicated, and also every aspect of the perceptual and affectual projections of the patient toward the therapist; the counterprojections, from the therapist to the patient, have come to be called "countertransference." It should be pointed out that in contemporary psychoanalytic theory and in recent clinical practice, "transference" and "countertransference" have assumed an expanded set of applications, beyond anything Freud recognized in his more limited sense of "transference."[8] Among the many applications of the terms in recent theory, one is of particular interest to this study. "Transference" may refer to the relationship of patients to the objects which have been of crucial importance to their psychological development. The precise nature of those object relationships becomes clear through the transference relationship between patient and therapist, and the subsequent working through of the relationship, so that a deeper understanding of objects and their powers in the psychic life (conscious and unconscious) of the patient emerges from the process of therapy between individuals.

If we are to extend the psychoanalytic concept of transference to the realm of cultural objects we must introduce developmental processes and sequences that go beyond the psychosexual as Freud dealt with them in clinical practice. The process of transference with cultural objects is complex, for the objects themselves are representational—that is, they too present and express transference relationships, to which the person regarding the object then in turn responds. We have a process that is like one of "mirroring," reverberating and reflecting back and forth through several layers of consciousness: the "consciousness" of the object; of the artist, who as it were makes a presentation of self through the object or in the object; and of the beholder, who responds to all the layers with an accumulation of conscious and unconscious associations which include deeply private nodal points in the unique developmental experience to which there are correspondences, but not identities, in others. Thus transference in regard to cultural objects possesses a historical as well as a psychosexual dimension. The benefits to the theory of balancing the two aspects of cultural experience will become evident in the examples presented below.

One consequence of extending the connotations of "tranference" is that the theory can more readily accommodate itself to a property of art that has been neglected in psychoanalytic concentration upon the single object. Just as the person has a past in terms of which the transference and countertransference relationships in the clinical setting are given specific form and content, so the relationship between person and object in the cultural tradition establishes the object-past of the objects as a *tradition of objects* whose interrelationship to a present perceived object functions as a background of reference and association. There is, therefore, a historical presence in two senses in the ways a person and an object, as it were, "see each other": there is the history of the object, and there is the history of the individual.

Freud concentrated on the history of the individual; the art historian concentrates on the history of the object. My aim in this study is to balance the two approaches so that individual and object are seen together under a clarified and expanded psychoanalytic model of explanation. The basic model of psychoanalytic explanation in the classical formulation was the clinical exchange between patient and therapist. And it was assumed that the model could be extended to artist and audience. In making an explanatory move of this kind, the model must be expanded and repositioned, as I am suggesting in the present reconsideration of transference. (Further discussion of transference will be presented in chapter 4, section II.)

In reading Freud's writings on culture there is always the question of how far he himself realized the deficiencies of the theory in its larger cultural applications. It seems to me that at first Freud took the relationship between individual and object in culture to be like the relationship between patient and dream, fantasy, parent, therapist. In keeping close to the analogy it became apparent that adequate interpretation of cultural objects was not achieved. But in later elaborations and reconsiderations Freud did come to see the importance of tradition in the understanding of cultural objects, so that with the familiarity of psychoanalytic interpretations growing and drawing to them more and more attention, a process was set in motion that was in some respects like, but in basic respects different from, the therapeutic process. A "cultural transference," if I may so refer to it, occurred as objects became more fully integrated into the conscious awareness of individuals through interpretations of the psychoanalytic kind.[9]

If the concept of transference is placed in the larger historical setting of a tradition of objects, we can expand the psychoanalytic idea of transference in the direction of a cultural and historical sense, yet keep the basic notion of a relationship between two interacting conscious and unconscious representations. "Transference" then refers to the ways in which the artist reacts to, makes use of, reinterprets, and restructures aesthetically the tradition within which work is carried out. Countertransference can of course be applied to the artist also, but I would prefer to consider "countertransference" as a relationship between audience and individually presented work, for the beholder responds to the *artist's* transference to the tradition. Turning now to the object, we can think of it as a cultural focus of transference and countertransference responses and interpretations on the part of generations of beholders. The implications of this way of seeing transference tie psychoanalytic theory all the more closely to the tradition of idealistic theories of art, a tradition, I argued in the previous chapter, to which the theory belongs. Seeing transference and countertransference as central to the experience of cultural objects identifies the psychoanalytic theory of interpretation with the interpretation it produces, so that Freud's method of interpretation, like Hegel's method of interpretation, constitutes the theory itself. Put briefly, the philosophic method is coextensive with the product.

If we regard psychoanalytic theory through the comparison to idealistic theories as a class, we can see its evolution toward the identification of method and product. After the theory had been established, Freud applied it as itself the possessor of implications for an understanding of culture which it itself had brought into consciousness through its own interpretations. Just as the theory in the clinical situation was able to give a sense to the ways patients possessed a developmental relationship to objects, so in the cultural situation the theory was presumed to cast light upon the historical past whose representations through art, myth, and folktale implied a developmental trajectory that could be interpreted as a possession of culture.

This analogy suggests the complex and multifarious ways meaning emerges in the process of interpretation, depending upon whether the focus of attention is upon the individual or upon the tradition in its grander sweep. In general, Freud took the position that in both the more confined and in the broader sweep, unconscious thought is represented in consciousness by means of symbols that are produced by severe condensation and by far-reaching displacement. In both dreams and art, the manifest must be taken as only the starting point for interpretation, and if we are to understand cultural objects we must find a like interpretative way from the manifest to the latent, and that way lies through the symbols which are *representations* of unconscious material. Representations, as Freud called them, are like compacted elements of the unconscious material which appear, not in any available or clearly understandable way, in the manifest content of objects. The task of interpretation is to get from the slight bits of evidence in the conscious dream or object to the unconscious dream-thought or object-thought (my phrase) which both generated the manifest content and endowed it with meaning, much of which remains to be reconstituted.

Art works, like all cultural products, are organized in a manifest, conscious way, and also in a latent, unconscious way. To discover the unconscious, latent content we must come to know how it is indicated, symbolized, and obliquely referred to by the manifest content. Such a statement of principles and method characterizes the theories of art I have classified as *expressionist* theories. Both Hegel and Freud developed interpretative methods to carry out the translation from manifest to latent. Both ask of cultural products, "What do they mean?" And both answer that they yield up their meaning upon application of the correct method of interpretation. Although the assumptions of the two methods differ, the basic principle of manifest and latent governs both procedures. They assume that the creative work of the artist must involve both conscious and unconscious elements of the artist's own psychic organization; and both attempt to demonstrate the human response to cultural products also functions in a conscious and an unconscious way.

The tension between conscious and unconscious responses in the perceiver, expressed in feelings of curiosity, anxiety, and incompleteness, is the affective basis for a continuing interpretative effort. Both Hegel and Freud thought of cultural objects as perpetually under analysis, although they differ, as I have already noted, in their concern for the grander historical events that shape human consciousness. But as far as Freud was concerned, the forces of the unconscious are irresistible.

III Psychoanalytic theory posits two forces as responsible for the hindrance and difficulty we find when we try to move from manifest to latent content in human products such as dreams and art. But the recurrent resistance to establishing semantic and syntactic relationships (speaking metaphorically) in the presented object is not simply a function of strangeness or incompleteness; sometimes the presentations are perceived as fragmentary and incomplete, and at other times they are experienced with intense pleasure and joyous exuberance. I think it should be emphasized that the two forces Freud thought responsible for the difficulty in moving from manifest to latent are at work both in the case of objects that seem compatible, consonant with ourselves (in psychoanalytic terms, "ego-syntonic"), and of objects that feel disjointed and incompatible (in psychoanalytic terms, "ego-dystonic"). The two forces at work in all cases of interpretation Freud referred to as "repression" and "overdetermination" (*Verdrängung* and *Über-determinierung*). They were postulated to be psychic forces whose dynamisms accounted for the withholding of meaning, the camouflage of meaning, and the often seemingly excessive complexity of meaning in the things human beings create. If ego-controlled meaning is to emerge as a consequence of interpretation, the mechanisms and the devious intricacies of the forces must be understood. In brief, the conclusions Freud reached in his effort to establish reliable interpretation are the following.

Repression has several manifestations, both structurally and developmentally. In the process of growing up, an original, early condition of repression is postulated by Freud. He writes,

We have reason to assume that there is a *primal repression,* a first phase of repression, which consists in the psychical (ideational) representative of the instinct being denied entrance into the conscious. With this a *fixation* is established; the representative in question persists unaltered from then onwards and the instinct remains attached to it.[10]

Early in the developmental sequence, Freud postulated, there are repressions which in effect substitute one idea, one specific awareness, for the appropriate idea that never was able to rise to consciousness because of repression, which kept it out of consciousness. What *did* get into consciousness was a substitute, which retains forever the instinctual affect that attached to its original, and for which it became the surrogate.

The theory of primal repression suggests an interesting interpretation of this phase of maturation for our understanding of art. An understanding of art has to do essentially with the ways works of art are made meaningful to the perceiver. "Representative" and "instinct . . . attached to it" can be given an *aesthetic* interpretation, for works of art share in the psychic reality of development; they exhibit exactly the persistence of element and affect that primal repression refers to.

Primal repression creates "fixations," that is, objects and words—peculiar to each psychic history—which receive strong, enduring affects that persist and become the focus of repetitions. Every artistic style, and each personal artistic history, possesses an organization of meaningful elements that go back to primal repression; but how the fixations develop is not clear. Their towardness is, however, clear in the elements that function as important nodes in a net of artistic structure throughout the career of the artist.

Characteristically, the deepest elements which primal repression fixates can be detached from any one specific context and moved to others. This underlies the metaphoric organization of the arts. Thus I propose a generalization: metaphoric elements and metaphoric inferences can often be traced back to deep, early primal repression. And, therefore, those elements take on a peculiar forcefulness in the work of an individual artist.

However, in reconstructing the concept of primal repression for the purposes of psychoanalytic theory as an explanation of art, I do not want to imply that the presence of primal repression reduces art to a symptom. The theory has often been accused of making that kind of reduction. Rather, primal repression works throughout the lifelong productivity of the artist as an expression of character (not symptom), which is apprehended by the audience through the developing and changing *style* of the works, and the deepening insights into the works provided by the style.

On the basis of this interpretation of primal repression, the concept of *iconography* can be extended: where the iconographic elements in art are traditionally limited to discriminable objects that have been given a specific meaning through a tradition of artistic reference, the phrase "iconography of the medium" extends the sense of the iconographic. "Iconography of the medium" refers to stylistic organization and repetition, colors, lines, phonetic and phonemic patterns, tonal organization, and all the elements of the various media themselves in their purely aesthetic immediacy. The medium itself functions as a structured object whose elements possess iconographic significance. While we often cannot translate the iconography of the medium into assertions of the sort that explicate thought, we can identify organizing structures essential to the art work and sometimes, through the careful consideration of evidence from a large body of work and from information about the artist, apply the concept of primal repression.

Primal repression now becomes a concept in psychoanalytic theory *of art*. A concept that was proposed to help explain the developmental phases in early childhood has been enlarged to help explain elements in the objects artists make. I am not suggesting that the elements can be understood in terms of the artists' development, for the psychodynamics of that process may be lost, or too difficult to reconstruct from the fragmented, and even on occasion unintegrated, elements in the objects. But we often can become aware of the artist's effort to realize character through a struggle to achieve developmental coherence.

Whatever the particular case, I am suggesting that the affective power we find in aesthetic elements—especially stylistic elements—derives its power and frequency of occurrence from early primal repression. In some few cases the original repressed ideation may be recovered.[11]

"Repression" has a second sense, more general and more obvious, the sense in which we use it today as a common term to describe the psychic force mobilized by the ego that prevents dangerous thoughts from reaching consciousness; the thoughts are dangerous because they pose a threat to the ego and the superego. In the normal course of psychic development, defenses must be thrown up against threatening wishes and beliefs because punishment may result from acting on them, but even more important, their expression would entail loss of love and loss of self-esteem. As a person grows up, impulses, wishes, drives are repressed; though they will find expression elsewhere, they cannot be directly and immediately expressed without consequent pain and anxiety.

Repression, a psychological mechanism and a concept playing a central role in psychoanalytic theory, came to be, in Freud's view, "the cornerstone on which the whole structure of analysis rests."[12] By implication, then, the mechanism and the concept will be discovered to be essential in the making and using of enactments. Objects created by humans, responded to by humans, will exhibit the force of repression in both the content of the objects and in the processes of response to the objects. In general, this means that objects still possess a latent content whose translation to manifest content will be at once sought and resisted. Just how the tension between the urgency toward recovery and the force of repression will be recognized led to some remarkable observations. In the essay "Repression," Freud referred to repression as "a preliminary stage of condemnation."[13] And this idea, that repression constitutes a form of value judgment that intimately affects the person, is elaborated in a later essay, "Negation," whose observations are central to an understanding of cultural objects.

In "Negation" Freud joins clinical observation to rhetorical structures: when a patient says no, denies the importance of a report of a memory, refuses to acknowledge the truth of an assertion, there are grounds for suspecting repression.[14] A negative judgment in some cases is the intellectual substitute for repression and indicates that the defense of repression is in force. This observation has interesting implications for interpretation of cultural objects, for negation, and its metaphoric representations, are used in subtle and powerful ways to structure the meanings of objects.

In discussing negation, Freud made a distinction, though not with sufficient firmness, between denial (*Verneinung*) and disavowal (*Verleugnung*). The distinction has importance in both the assessment of the statements made by a patient, and in our interpretation of the sentences of a text. When a patient in analysis uses a negation, the negative may be a denial, or it may be a disavowal. A sentence may be judged simply not true; or a sentence may be one that provokes anxiety, and one from which the patient must disengage. The use of negation in the generic sense does not in itself determine whether an assertion is a denial or a disavowal. It is up to the clinical investigator to determine whether the patient is simply making a judgment, or taking a particular position that has consequences for therapy.

A similar problem confronts the reader of a text in which negation occurs in problematical ways. Both denial and disavowal function in complex ways when the stance of the text, or the speaker in a text, is not obvious. For example, a novel, such as *The Confidence Man* by Herman Melville, opens with a narrative technique that suggests the paradox of the liar. That is, the speaker produces (in this case writes) sentences whose truth value is indeterminate, for they are the utterances of a liar who says, in effect, that what I say is true. Since he is a liar, when he claims truthfulness we suspect falsehood; when falsehood, we suspect truth. The consequence for the novel is destructive; to every claim made in the novel we are driven to the doubt of indeterminacy, unable to assign a truth value to the sentences. However, even though *The Confidence Man* is a text in the narrative grip of indeterminacy, prolonged and intimate acquaintance with the book gives grounds for interpretation and the sorting out of truths and falsehoods. But here as with the utterances of the consulting room, careful analysis and interpretation must be applied to negation in all its manifestations.

Freud made further observations on the way repression works. The force of repression tends to spread, to affect events, beliefs, wishes, needs that are related to the original focus of repression. Repression contaminates thought, it "proliferates in the dark," and therefore compels elements of the object to enter into its work. The consequence of the seepage of repression, if we can think of it that way, is to allow elements related to the original repressed material entrance into consciousness depending upon their distance from the original. Interpretation must therefore determine the techniques for both separating elements from repression and relating elements to repression, but in such a way that the manifest can allow inferential connections to the center of repression to be made. The concept of repression emphasizes the interdependence and interrelationship of an array of elements whose meaningful connection is through a force that surrounds them in a way analogous to a magnetic field.[15] Thus repression draws material into its field of force, as it were, and also, as with all psychological processes, can move about and appear in different places and in different guises in the life history of an individual.

The same applies to repression as it manifests itself in objects, objects as created things representing repressed events and processes, and objects as things responded to by a culture which accepts and rejects various repressed subjects. Where repression occurs, of course, a degree of feeling attaches to the objects and the experiences we have of the objects. Repression accounts for feeling in two senses: it both inhibits and encourages, but the feelings it generates can be responses to feelings inhibited. Thus, though repression has not figured in philosophies of art outside the psychoanalytic, it seems to be a useful concept in the philosophy of art generally, for it offers a subtle, sensitive analysis of feelings as they are orchestrated in the object.

It would not be correct to think that there is no recognition of repression in the arts as they have been understood before psychoanalytic theory explored and defined the mechanisms of defense. One important use of something like the psychoanalytic conception of repression in classical textual exegesis has always been to separate the artist from an inspiring force outside the artist. That the muse might make her own use of art was an exciting idea, and suggested even artists might not know all that their art expressed. To merge artist and muse, and translate the inspiring force from without to within, destroys a myth of externalization, but succeeds in putting the artist in direct relationship and responsibility to the work produced.

Psychoanalytic theory not only attributes a multitude of sources—conscious and unconscious—to the artist; it goes further to postulate "overdetermination" for actions, so that in the case of artistic creativity, multiple grounds for every aspect of a work of art are predicted. Detailed biographical studies of artists have discovered the difficulty in assigning a single cause to a work, or to a part of a work; it seems that there are always multiple, coexisting determining factors that are necessarily effective in explaining an action, a fantasy, a dream, a work of art. Several explanations, all relevant, may be given to explain why an artist uses specific words, gestures, images, thoughts, and chooses as well a specific way to communicate them. What is excluded from consciousness, as well as that which appears in consciousness, can be given several explanations, for psychic events have multiple causes, and the causes, though coming together to produce a single event, must be disentangled and seen in their cumulative efficacy. It follows from the psychoanalytic concept of overdetermination that psychological interpretation is not to be exhausted in one account, and in this respect also psychoanalytic explanations are like the Hegelian interpretative method, for both assume that inquiry into and interpretation of cultural events are interminable.

The application of this principle of continuous interpretation to works of art is obvious. Both that which finds its way into, and that which is left out of a work of art, call for explanation. And since the presences and absences are overdetermined, the things said about a work of art cannot be the exclusive possession of one mind, one method, one explanation. Several explanatory systems may apply to a work of art, and a single response to a work of art will be but one of several different, yet within definable limits, appropriate, responses. Multiplicity of interpretations and responses follows from the assumption of the manifest–latent distinction, since the degree of penetration into latent material, and the comprehensibility of the interpretation, depend upon the respondent's ability to bring together the manifest and the latent content into a coherent account. The greater the integration of manifest and latent material, the more likely a satisfactory interpretation of powerful feelings produced by the object will be achieved.

In one respect, as has been noted, psychoanalytic interpretation is ahistorical, for it carries on the analysis of cultural objects without, as a rule, attending to the time and place of origin. In another respect, however, psychoanalytic interpretation is—if not historical—at least temporal, for it sees responses to art as functions of the perceiver's maturation and growing sensitivity to latent content. The development of the person from infancy to adulthood, though hardly the vast range of cultural history that so intrigued Hegel, is the focus of a narrative equally complex. In some ways, it seems to me, Freud's conception of maturation and growth is like that of the American philosopher John Dewey, for both emphasize the vicissitudes of the ego's interaction with the psychic and cultural environment. Freud's psychological world exhibits a kind of ahistorical constancy that removes the maturation of the person from the waywardness of historical change. This does not mean, however, that the history of the individual is free from serious upheavals; although one cannot explain and understand neurosis and psychosis in the usual historical terms, it is of course true that the conflicts exhibited by individuals in their creative lives may be exacerbated by accidents of fate, and therefore a psychoanalytic account of art may find it necessary to refer to historical events.

Neglect of history must include the tradition of art itself, and on that particular design in the great tapestry of the past psychoanalytic theory of art is becoming more and more art-historical. It is now recognized, through the writings of Ernst Kris, Heinz Hartmann, Otto Kernberg, and many others that primary process thinking is indeed itself a part of the developmental process, and that a thoroughgoing developmentalism is obliged to consider the impact of historical continuities upon both conscious and unconscious thought. These issues will be given further consideration in the chapters to come.

IV There is a major effort made by psychoanalytic theory to understand how the psychic life of the individual becomes mobilized in such a way that products which exhibit a manifest and a latent content come into existence. I shall give a brief description of this part of the theory, for it introduces two concepts of central importance to the interpretation of art: the "primary process" and the "secondary process."

Thought begins chronologically with the organization of ideas in a way that Freud characterized as the "primary process," which he conceived as under the guidance of a principle of mental functioning to which he gave the name "pleasure principle." The primary process he considered an activity of the id, and he believed that this kind of thinking was organized differently from that found in conscious thought.

We have found that processes in the unconscious or in the id obey different laws from those in the preconscious ego. We name these laws in their totality the *primary process*, in contrast to the *secondary process*, which governs the course of events in the preconscious, in the ego.[16]

Secondary process thinking, in contrast, proceeds under the guidance of what Freud referred to as the "reality principle," whose aim is to accommodate to, and develop an ability to cope with, the external world. Together, primary process and secondary process exhaust the processes of thought and they together must account for products such as art.[17]

It is in this part of the theory that some of the most interesting possibilities for a psychoanalytic theory of art still rest, and in my opinion remain to be exploited.

According to psychoanalytic theory, all works of art will exhibit and be organized in terms of these two mental processes in various combinations. Great art will somehow grapple with primary process thinking, both to use it and to refer to it in its manifest content. Just how the artist succeeded in doing this Freud believed to be a secret that psychoanalysis could not unlock. When artists do find ways of representing primary process thinking, their work opens up to us wide ranges of the unconscious that we, unaided, would never be able to encounter. On the other hand, art produced under rigid ego control— art produced under the domination of the secondary process— may also reveal primary process thought, but in forms that make interpretation more difficult. Even psychotic art, whose facade often strikes us as impenetrable, can be interpreted through psychoanalytic theory, for it discovers the fantasy system in terms of which the art was produced. I shall discuss an interpretation of this kind at the beginning of chapter 4.

V As Freud's theory of psychic life became more developed and as it grew in complexity following the papers of the early 1920s, the analysis of art was neglected in the sense that theory outstripped practice. There is little effort to apply the later theoretical formulations to art, so that one might say as far as psychoanalytic writing on art was concerned Freud remained content with fixation at an early level. Yet his theory promises a great deal more for our understanding than he himself realized, and I shall now briefly discuss the implications of some of the later thought for our understanding of art.

In the postscript to "An Autobiographical Study" Freud says that his later years found him returning to several of his earliest interests:

My interest, after making a long *détour* through the natural sciences, medicine and psychotherapy, returned to the cultural problems which had fascinated me long before, when I was a youth, scarcely old enough for thinking. At the very climax of my psycho-analytic work in 1912, I had already attempted in *Totem and Taboo* to make use of the newly discovered findings of analysis in order to investigate the origins of religion and morality. I now carried this work a stage further in two later essays, *The Future of an Illusion,* and *Civilization and Its Discontents.* I perceived ever more clearly that the events of human history, the interactions between human nature, cultural development and the precipitates of primaeval experiences (the most prominent example of which is religion) are no more than a reflection of the dynamic conflicts between the ego, the id and the super-ego, which psycho-analysis studies in the individual—are the very same processes repeated upon a wider stage.[18]

The reflections on religion and culture to which Freud refers are relevant to the extension of his thought upon art, but the connection between the cultural and the aesthetic theory was not made by Freud himself, and really was not pressed by his followers, although Paul Ricoeur and Herbert Marcuse have seen the interconnection. As I shall argue below, in chapter 3, I believe a general theory of cultural life can be generated from Freud's thought. Yet there is a perplexing lack in Freud's own writing on the cultural aspects of the objects produced in a tradition.

One of the most difficult questions left unexplored in Freud's later reflections on art is this: What explanation would psychoanalytic theory offer of the cultural uses and functions of art? In reading *Civilization and Its Discontents* we are mindful of the fact that works of art themselves often are concerned with the very same issues raised by Freud's essay. We are then led to ask, Is the content of such works relevant to Freud's speculation? And, we must ask, does Freud himself attempt to answer this question? *Civilization and Its Discontents* suggests that we ought to reconsider the earlier writings, and when we do, we come to see that the late essay does make a contribution to Freud's early writing, and to the general nature of art as a cultural product.

As Freud's ruminations on the shape of his intellectual career point out, his life work had as its goal the integration of conclusions of the clinic, contained in his case histories and his metapsychological speculations, with his imaginative reconstructions of the human past and the inevitable conflicts that history bequeaths to the cultural present. A psychoanalytic theory of art must aim at a like integration, and to that unfinished work of Freud's late writing we can now turn.

Appendix

The distinction we have made between the two psychical systems receives fresh significance when we observe that processes in the one system, the *Ucs.*, show characteristics which are not met with again in the system immediately above it.

The nucleus of the *Ucs.* consists of instinctual representatives which seek to discharge their cathexis; that is to say, it consists of wishful impulses. These instinctual impulses are coordinate with one another, exist side by side without being influenced by one another, and are exempt from mutual contradition. When two wishful impulses whose aims must appear to us incompatible become simultaneously active, the two impulses do not diminish each other or cancel each other out, but combine to form an intermediate aim, a compromise.

There are in this system no negation, no doubt, no degrees of certainty: all this is only introduced by the work of the censorship between the *Ucs.* and the *Pcs.* Negation is a substitute, at a higher level, for repression. In the *Ucs.* there are only contents, cathected with greater or lesser strength.

The cathectic intensities [in the *Ucs.*] are much more mobile. By the process of *displacement* one idea may surrender to another its whole quota of cathexis; by the process of *condensation* it may appropriate the whole cathexis of several other ideas. I have proposed to regard these two processes as distinguishing marks of the so-called *primary psychical process*. In the system *Pcs.* the *secondary process* is dominant. When a primary process is allowed to take its course in connection with elements belonging to the system *Pcs.*, it appears "comic" and excites laughter.

The processes of the system *Ucs.* are *timeless;* i.e. they are not ordered temporally, are not altered by the passage of time; they have no reference to time at all. Reference to time is bound up, once again, with the work of the system *Cs.*

The *Ucs.* processes pay just as little regard to *reality*. They are subject to the pleasure principle; their fate depends only on how strong they are and on whether they fulfil the demands of the pleasure–unpleasure regulation.

To sum up: *exemption from mutual contradiction, primary process* (mobility of cathexes), *timelessness*, and *replacement of external by psychical reality*—these are the characteristics which we may expect to find in processes belonging to the system *Ucs.*

Unconscious processes only become cognizable by us under the conditions of dreaming and of neurosis—that is to say, when processes of the higher, *Pcs.*, system are set back to an earlier stage by being lowered (by regression). In themselves they cannot be cognized, indeed are even incapable of carrying on their existence; for the system *Ucs.* is at a very early moment overlaid by the *Pcs.* which has taken over access to consciousness and to motility. (From "The Unconscious," Std. Ed., 14: 186–187)

III

Psychoanalytic Theory
of Culture

Psychoanalytic theory of interpretation evolved from the general theory of psychosexual development and its clinical base, the study of dreams. From the interpretation of dreams, the interpretation of art and cultural products followed. In this chapter, a psychoanalytic theory of culture will be elaborated, and a proposal made to complement the traditional psychoanalytic concepts as they are applied to art with the philosophical concept of *enactment*.

I The cultural writings of Freud have long been considered his most speculative contributions, and in recent years the attacks upon them have intensified. Yet they are fundamental to psychoanalytic theory of art and culture, often in ways that Freud himself failed to see, or at least to make use of in his own thinking. And despite the highly speculative nature of the cultural writings, Freud's followers have clarified some of his ideas, again without being fully aware of the accomplishment and the significance for a theory of art. Hence my task here is twofold: I shall criticize the shortcomings of Freud's writings on culture, and at the same time attempt to demonstrate their positive, and indeed extremely useful, contribution to the theory as a whole.

The cultural writings of Freud have come under attack in

recent years: not only is he considered to have relied upon out-moded anthropology—the work of Frazer and Goldenweiser, Tylor and Westermarck—but also his own stories of the human past are considered bizarre and without foundation. Hence the two major anthropological books, *Totem and Taboo* and *Moses and Monotheism,* have been put aside as curiosities. It is my intention to take another look at these books. I believe there are fundamental points made in them which led later thinkers to develop useful conceptions of how cultural objects function at different levels of maturation.

In a talk given in honor of James Strachey, D. W. Winnicott said:

Freud did not have a place in his topography of the mind for the experience of things cultural. He gave new value to inner psychic reality, and from this came a new value for things that are actual and truly external. Freud used the word "sublimation" to point the way to the place where cultural experience is meaningful, but perhaps he did not get so far as to tell us where in the mind cultural experience is.[1]

Although Winnicott goes on to develop a theory of cultural events, he is content to leave the views of Freud as described; there is no criticism made of the psychoanalytic tradition beyond that. Yet at the time Winnicott made his remarks, the tradition was under persistent attack. The attacks made at that time failed, I believe, to see the basic aims of Freud's anthropological writing, and I shall attempt to say what the aims were in *Totem and Taboo* and in *Moses and Monotheism.*

In *Totem and Taboo* Freud attempted to construct a general theory of *Weltanschauungen;* in *Moses and Monotheism* he attempted, in a Kantian manner, to answer the question "How is culture possible?" Viewed in this way, Freud's books can be seen as standing in a philosophical tradition going back to Kant and Hegel.

I do not know if Freud himself recognized the philosophical

sources of his arguments, but he was aware of the problem of *Weltanschauung*, for he commented in the thirty-fifth "lecture" of *New Introductory Lectures on Psychoanalysis* that "a depth-psychology or psychology of the unconscious—is quite unfit to construct a Weltanschauung of its own: it must accept the scientific one."[2] As the argument proceeds, Freud refers to Kant and to Marx. Although Hegel is not referred to, the general discussion of the place of a *Weltanschauung* in modern thought assumes the idealistic reflections which followed from the Hegelian inquiry into culture. In a general philosophical respect, then, this lecture demonstrates a sensitive awareness to the kinds of issues that lay behind the thought of *Totem and Taboo* and of *Moses and Monotheism*. But the easy identification of psychoanalysis with the *Weltanschauung* of science— as Freud understood it—is misleading. A more accurate identification would be with the tradition of both empiricistic and idealistic philosophy.

There is a further continuity between nineteenth-century philosophy and psychoanalytic theory as established by Freud, for both kinds of explanation—the philosophical and the psychoanalytic—are deeply concerned to give an account of objects and the relationship between persons and objects. In this respect, as well as in respect to explanations of the epistemological sort discussed in the last chapter, psychoanalytic theory complements and enlarges philosophical visions. Philosophers were inspired and energized by an essentially Newtonian conception of physical objects and saw the relationship between persons and objects in terms of perception and the gathering of evidence. So, too, psychoanalytic theory was inspired by the Newtonian vision now as a model for the search inward, imagining a hidden inner analogous to the hidden outer of science. But that was only the rather rote beginning of a psychoanalytic theory of objects, for the outer world was to be understood in terms not simply of objects perceived but rather of objects loved, hated, highly charged emotionally with a great variety of feelings, and in general—to use the term which unfortunately came to be the English translation of the German *Besetzung*—objects highly "cathected." So from very early on, psychoanalytic theory considered objects in a special way that we shall study.

I shall argue that the theory of objects in Freud's cultural writing establishes a foundation for the more empirical, clinical treatment of objects to be found in the clinical papers, and also provides essential ideas for Freud's followers as they further develop the theory of objects. I shall then go on to argue that the psychoanalytic theory of objects, as set forth in the anthropological books, is incomplete, and that the analysis of objects and the relations between persons and objects requires the introduction of a class of objects I shall call "enactments."

I will begin with the earliest attempt at anthropology, *Totem and Taboo*. All of the later essays on human prehistory, as well as the speculations on the contradictions of civilization, go back to *Totem and Taboo*. Freud regarded it as a fundamental statement, and never gave up its findings, though they were sharply criticized.

The general theory of *Weltanschauung* that Freud proposed is this: the earliest human model of explanation of nature was animism, a theory that rests upon a basic human need and belief, the omnipotence of thought. Animism is also a primitive cultural attempt to explain dreams, the first attempt to do that which is finally fully achieved in *The Interpretation of Dreams*. Further, since *Weltanschauungen* subsequent to animism—that is, religion and science—are also expressions of a belief in the omnipotence of thought, Freud argued that all stages in the human effort to give an explanation of nature rest on a condition that psychoanalysis has investigated with great thoroughness.

There is, Freud implied, a deep affinity between the earliest human explanation and the latest, between animism and psychoanalysis. In between these two stages of the development of human explanatory theory, there occur religion and science. The implication is clear: the history of human thought exhibits four stages of a dialectical process, each stage of which constitutes a *Weltanschauung*. They are (1) animism, (2) religion, (3) science, (4) psychoanalytic theory. This sequence displays interesting parallels to both the Hegelian and the Comtean philosophical interpretations of the stages of human thought. Freud would agree with Hegel that the final stage of development we know—for Freud that would be modern science—expresses a higher, more inclusive, and more self-conscious level of consciousness which can be used to interpret earlier stages of thought, which in the truly Hegelian sense of "dialectic" are taken up into later stages. Freud would agree with Comte that the present condition of human inquiry succeeds insofar as it frees itself from the limitations, myths, and misunderstandings of the earlier stages. Although Freud would not have been as simplistic as Comte, they would have shared a general belief in the human capacity to extend the powerful method of science to the interpretation of all human activities, and in the light of present awareness, to reinterpret the past stages of thought that Comte classified as "theological" and "metaphysical." Like his predecessors, Freud was committed to the interpretation of all cultural products by a unified method.

Despite Freud's belief that his method was scientific and expressed the world view of science, the method he worked out is more philosophical than scientific, even though the clinical procedure is thoroughly empirical. It is clear from the texts themselves that Freud thought of his work—however much inspired by science—as original in its method, and philosophical in its speculative scope. The degree to which he was aware that the four stages of development outlined in *Totem and Taboo* suggest an idealistic dialectical structure we simply do not know.

Each stage of human thought, Freud argued, expressed the human need to believe in the omnipotence of thought. At the animistic stage, human beings assign omnipotence to themselves; at the religious stage, they assign power to the gods and preserve a bit of precarious influence to humans; at the scientific stage humans assign no power to themselves as agents, but great power to thought that understands the force of nature and natural necessity. With this humans possess a recognition of the inevitability of mortality. The final stage, psychoanalysis, endows humans with superior insight, and develops to the full the capacity to cut through illusion and false belief. Above all, psychoanalysis enriches the scientific method with a humanistic power of interpretation. Thus, although psychoanalysis is a science, it can turn its scrutiny onto science itself, and therefore has had the power to liberate human thought from the trammels that science, as a simple natural philosophy, cannot understand because it has not achieved—and cannot achieve—self-consciousness sufficient to a critique of its own assumptions. Freud believed that one of the characteristics of psychoanalytic method was its capacity to discover its own latent thought and bring it into manifest awareness.

Applying his own method to the stages of human development, Freud made explicit the power of psychoanalytic method to interpret the past. First, *Weltanschauungen,* he argued, express varying degress of sexualization of thought; second, every *Weltanschauung* exhibits two reasons for its structure, one a seemingly rational system with premises many of which will be found to be delusional. The other reasons are concealed (unconscious), but are the truly operative ones. The latter provide the conceptual motive power of the system. Every stage of thought exhibits a manifest and a latent system of thought; only the psychoanalytic method can dig them out and separate them.

Looked at in this way, the theses of *Totem and Taboo* appear to be speculative in a philosophical way, quite in the manner of post-Hegelian idealism, and therefore part of a tradition that, through the development of disciplines such as art history, has come to be central to the way we regard and interpret cultural objects. Indeed, our own humanistic disciplines today partici-

pate in many of the assumptions that underlie Freud's speculations, for not only has the activity of interpretation itself become a central focus in those studies we call "humanities," but
the very activity of interpretation itself has been taken by some
to be an independent subject.

I shall now turn to the two discoveries Freud claimed to have
made in regard to the nature of human thought in its several
stages. The first is that every stage exhibits a specific, definable sexualization of thought; the second, that every stage will
exhibit a set of conscious premises, in part delusional, and a
set of concealed reasons that are the truly operative, conceptually motivating part of the *Weltanschauung*.

The first discovery is consistent with the theory of sexuality
developed in the *Three Essays on the Theory of Sexuality*. I
believe that Freud was arguing for a parallel development between the psychosexual stages of human maturation and the
stages of *Weltanschauungen*. I will explore briefly the assertion
that this parallelism, when articulated, contributes to an understanding of culture. Freud's statement is this:

> If we may regard the existence among primitive races of the om-
> nipotence of thoughts as evidence in favour of narcissism, we are
> encouraged to attempt a comparison between the phases in the de-
> velopment of men's view of the universe and the stages of an individ-
> ual's libidinal development. The animistic phase would correspond to
> narcissism both chronologically and in its content; the religious phase
> would correspond to the stage of object-choice of which the charac-
> teristic is a child's attachment to his parents; while the scientific
> phase would have an exact counterpart in the stage at which an in-
> dividual has reached maturity, has renounced the pleasure principle,
> adjusted himself to reality and turned to the external world for the
> object of his desires.
>
> In only a single field of our civilization has the omnipotence of
> thoughts been retained, and that is in the field of art. Only in art
> does it still happen that a man who is consumed by desires performs
> something resembling the accomplishment of those desires and that
> what he does in play produces emotional effects—thanks to artistic
> illusion—just as though it were something real. People speak with

justice of the 'magic of art' and compare artists to magicians. But the comparison is perhaps more significant than it claims to be. There can be no doubt that art did not begin as art for art's sake. It worked originally in the service of impulses which are for the most part extinct to-day. And among them we may suspect the presence of many magical purposes.[3]

Each stage in the developing *Weltanschauung* can be understood as a *cultural* manifestation of a psychosexual relationship between a person and external objects. Freud is here transferring to the cultural level of human behavior the dynamism of the maturational process. As far as I can understand this attempt at a theory, it is untenable; there is no way to verify it, and little evidence that can easily lead us to reject it. For that reason I will not make any argument concerning its scientific credibility or methodological sloppiness; rather I will see if anything can be done with it that might be useful in understanding cultural life.

Certainly we do not think that there is cultural homogeneity at each stage of a *Weltanschauung* in the sense that all people at that stage manifest the same degree of psychosexual maturity.

If there is any point to the parallel Freud drew, it is in the *location* of cultural objects in the communal life we find at each stage of a *Weltanschauung*. It is a point made by Dewey in his book *Art as Experience* (a book that is in many ways very Freudian, though antiseptically nonpsychoanalytic): that cultural behavior in regard to objects varies tremendously from preliterate, through early literate, to modern society. And I think Freud recognized something of this, though his exclusively psychological preoccupations made him put the insight into psychological terms, when it should have been put into anthropological or sociological terms.

Freud argued that culture moves from stage to stage as humans move from stage to stage psychosexually, and that preliminary *Weltanschauungen* are caused by the particular stage of psychosexual development the human race has attained at a particular time. But the hypothesis can be framed differently; the systems we call animism, religion, science are themselves sustained by all of the psychosexual stages, and the stages are probably phylogenetically fixed. There is no reason to postulate a set psychosexual orientation for each *Weltanschauung;* rather, there is every reason to suppose that the development of each *Weltanschauung* will exhibit the place for each psychosexual stage of development. We must look elsewhere in history and psychology for an answer to the question "Why did animism-religion give way to science?" To postulate a single cause, such as psychosexual maturational changes, is far too simple. The most we can say at this point is that an explanation of the sort Freud sought requires vast amounts of data, carefully scrutinized. Of course, it may be the case that in any one society, or at any one stage in the evolution of a society, the way objects are created, used, and regarded is in fact a function of the childhood experiences shared by all members of that society. But an anthropological and sociological analysis of the society at a particular time will reveal a variety of object relationships which have to be defined by age, by social position, and by responsibility. Freud's generalizations lack the sensitive differentiations that cross-cultural study requires.

At every stage of culture we will find artistic things functioning in *all* of the ways described by the analogy between *Weltanschauungen* and stages of psychosexual development. The "magic of art" is far more diverse than Freud admits, for every culture, whatever its degree of maturation, uses art in a variety of ways that express degrees of psychosexual development. And in the developmental trajectory of the individual, narcissistic gratification as well as the objectification of scientific outlook may well be found in the encounter with a particular work of art or enactment at different times, or at one and the same time. There is no contradiction in attributing concurrent gratifications of varying kinds to the individual's experience with works of art.

Objects that the culture "cathects" gratify psychologically in ways more complex than Freud's discussion of objects recognized, and no effort was made, curiously, to provide a developmental sketch of the ways an individual responds to and uses objects at the various linear psychosexual stages of maturation. It remains, therefore, to bring contemporary psychoanalytic theory of objects to bear on the psychoanalytic interpretation of art. I shall consider means to this integration in later sections of this chapter. It may be here remarked that Freud's own consideration of cultural objects moved from the level of the most intimate, individual concerns exhibited in the process of growing up, to the level of vast sweeps of cultural history, making little effort to relate the two disparate levels of development. I think that this discontinuity was in part responsible for the recognition, by recent theorists, of the need to return once more to objects in an effort to articulate a developmental theory embracing individual and cultural history.

In answer to the second question—how shall we discriminate a latent and a manifest content in *Weltanschauungen?*—the conclusion must be that the distinction requires us to go beyond the hasty answers given in psychoanalytic speculations on art and culture. Cultural life, to be understood, requires social and historical study. The disciplines now referred to as "psychohistory," "psychosociology," and "psychoanthropology" are efforts to integrate psychoanalytic thought with the findings of the social sciences. That development is in its initial stages but should be able to build upon the insights of early theory.

In *Moses and Monotheism* Freud asked the Kantian-like question "How is culture possible?" I think the method used to answer the question is also Kantian-like, because the argument works by a systematic presuppositional account, assuming that we can discover the conditions necessary and sufficient for culture by working back to a basic unconditioned foundation.

The first developmental event postulated is this: a necessary condition for the achievement of culture is the renunciation of exclusive reliance upon perception, and the emergence of thought. In Freud's conceptualization of development, this means that primary process thinking is succeeded, to a marked degree, by secondary process thinking, and that the ego and superego are in process of formation. The second condition postulated is the development of speech, making communication possible, and also the accumulation of memory, for speech and memory are functions of one another. Third, Freud assumed the condition of patriarchy must obtain, for it is the expression of a deep psychological change from perceptual to conceptual relationships to the world. With matriarchy (a condition Freud assumed to be the most primitive family organization) humans recognize the perceptual connection of mother and child. Once the role of the father in procreation is inferred, a higher, more abstract, and sophisticated system of concepts emerges into consciousness and that intellectual level of development is required for culture. As humans develop, Freud argued, they will necessarily organize themselves in a patriarchy, since the ability to comprehend that organization of society is a function of the developing capacity to think. Freud's views on patriarchy as a communal organization following from a cognitive advance is a point at which severe criticism would be directed today.

Animism, the fourth precondition for culture, establishes the first step toward systematic explanation of the sort we think of as science, although animism is full of magical thinking. However, with animism human beings achieve their first *Weltanschauung,* for animism relies upon language and constructs causal explanations. A *world* begins to emerge. I would add that the characteristics of this world include the organizing power of memory and also the appearance of meaningful repetitions, particularly the kinds of cultural events I shall refer to as "enactments."

The fifth precondition Freud postulated is the *Book*, a consolidation of narration and common belief into a system accepted as the true account of a people's origin and destiny. Psychoanalytic theory has not considered the Book an event requiring extended inquiry; but we can see that the Book is in one form or another—oral or written—a possession of every cultural tradition, and in terms of the argument to come in the next section, an *enactment*. Despite its neglect of this kind of cultural event, psychoanalytic theory has contributed indirectly to our understanding of events of this kind, and I shall enlarge upon those contributions.

Although Freud's contribution toward a theory of culture in *Moses and Monotheism* may seem to be slight, in two respects it makes a contribution: one is its stress upon the process of maturation in both culture and community life; the second is its attempt to state the conditions for the appearance of a *Weltanschauung*.

The Kantian-like method of presuppositional argument which Freud employs here is open to a number of objections, for in going from a given condition—in the case of *Moses and Monotheism*, that of culture—to the ground of its possibility, one can easily select the wrong set of logical and historical steps as the preconditions for the event one seeks to explain. The steps Freud chose are important, but not exhaustive; much more has to go on for human society as we know it to emerge. Yet the steps Freud chose are themselves reflected upon in every cultural account, in myth and legend, religion and ancestral tradition. By and large the cultural evidence itself supports the events described in *Moses and Monotheism* as fundamental to coherent cultural achievement. At least it can be said that Freud's argument identifies cultural presuppositions insofar as we know about them in stories of origin and destiny that are common to all traditions.

The lack in Freud's cultural theory is discovered when we attempt to understand cultural objects in their fullest functioning. The theory, rather than pursue the suggestions implicit in anthropological writings, shifts back to the kind of analysis we have already described in the preceding chapters. No account of cultural objects in the large sense demanded by art history and the philosophy of art emerges. In order to bring together and to make coherent the psychoanalytic treatment of art and the psychoanalytic treatment of culture, the psychoanalytic theory of objects must be developed.

II A psychoanalytic theory of objects was first adumbrated as early as the correspondence with Fliess, but achieved theoretical use in the early considerations of narcissism.[4] In the essay "On Narcissism" Freud writes, "An object is that to which a drive is directed." "Object" may refer to an external physical object, to a part of the body of the person, to a part of the body of another person, and to something entertained in fantasy. An object, however, is alwyas an object *for me*, psychoanalytically speaking, and all objects under this theory are positively, negatively, or neutrally cathected. In the life history of a person, objects play different roles, vary in cathected charge, and are subject to shifts in affective attention. An object that satisfies drives at one stage of development will not do so at a later stage, or may do so in a different context.

The psychoanalytic theory of objects directs attention to their representational nature: an "object" is an internal *representation* of an external or internal event, and therefore no matter how public the original, a psychoanalytic regard always sees the inner psychological reality through the outer physical reality, and their interdependence as a stage in a larger maturational sequence.

The philosophical tradition, in contrast, has tended to think of objects not developmentally, but as events having only a public history. This has led to many epistemological difficulties, solutions to which have been sought through philosophical analyses proposed by phenomenology and existentialism. Although in both of those recent efforts psychoanalytic thought has occasionally played a part, the psychoanalytic theory of objects has not been drawn upon to the extent that in my view would be useful and clarifying. It is especially in the domains of art and culture that a psychoanalytic theory of objects can help us to see the developmental complexities of the relationships between individuals and objects.

However, Freud never explicitly connected his theory of objects and the theory of culture stated in *Totem and Taboo* and in *Moses and Monotheism,* except in the following brief reflection on the psychosexual dynamics of the ego ideal in political life:

The ego ideal opens up an important avenue for the understanding of group psychology. In addition to its individual side, this ideal has a social side; it is also the common ideal of a family, a class or a nation. It binds not only a person's narcissistic libido, but also a considerable amount of homosexual libido, which is in this way turned back into ego.[5]

Freud goes on to explain the complex interplay of the ego ideal in political life, and calls our attention to the intense anxiety feelings connected to the maintenance of such an ideal. The anxiety often is transformed into guilt and acted out in politically destructive ways. Insofar as these feelings and actions are integral to social life, Freud did relate his theory of objects and his theory of culture. But it is a brief observation, and leaves out of account the vast range of objects sustained and responded to by the individual in the course of a life.

The ego ideals to which Freud refers are of course private and public modes of comportment, collections of qualities and characteristics that are models for the developing child, which persist in the superego as sources for criticism and exhortation in conduct. Freud does not pursue the observation that narcissism is the source of ego ideals, hence of cultural life in a very basic sense. To pursue it requires a search for the source of ego ideals, and in any culture they exist as much in narratives, rituals, folklore, tradition as they do in the immediate models of the parents, or whatever living persons are introjected in the formation of the superego—that is, of conscience. It is my contention that a psychoanalytic theory of culture calls for an elaboration and refinement of Freud's early investigation into objects.

There are two established sources for the effort I propose here: that is, a psychoanalytic theory of culture can draw upon the inquiry into narcissism, with all its later development and elaboration in the work of recent thinkers, and this would include the adaptation theory of Hartmann; and it can draw upon the psychoanalytic inquiry into art which also by now has a long history, and this would include the work of Klein, Winnicott, and Stokes.

Yet these sources are still incoherent and conceptually unrelated, so that in making use of them, we must supply our own formal organization and theoretical stance. I shall do that by organizing the various psychoanalytic sources and piecemeal observations under a cultural concept that I have found very useful, that of *enactment*. I turn now to a theory of enactment, building it up from the psychoanalytic sources referred to above.

Enactments are cultural events, objects, actions that are used, presented, and honored; they have a cultural status not unlike that of persons, though they are made things that can be classified in terms of their media. They are linguistic (both oral and written); material (made out of stuff, as paintings, sculptures, buildings); and tonal (sounds of the voice, instruments, natural noises). Enactments are so integral and basic to culture that I shall propose the following definition: *culture is a tradition of enactments.*

"Tradition" implies a set of interrelated objects whose functions and meanings depend upon one another as well as upon their individual structures. Their interdependence contributes to their capacity as cathected objects, for they share and induce affective force that finds deeply sympathetic responses in the audience trained in the tradition. Coordinate with the affective force is the formal structure of each object that can be learned, acquired, and passed on from generation to generation. The formal structure is usually referred to as "style," a term I shall use in a much broader sense to include the expressive, the affective, as well as the classifying characteristic of enactments. Style embraces both a mode of representation and a mode of expression, and indeed it has been claimed by some historians of cultural objects that stylistic affinities can be found in many different aspects of a culture's products: thought, action, object, even fantasy and dream, are claimed on occasion to possess deep structural affinities. Whether or not that can be objectively determined, whether or not stylistic affinities are perceived through simple constant association, we can assert that style makes the object, the person, the culture in a specific instantiation, and that our identification of our selves and our traditions takes place in large measure through stylistic familiarity and stylistic foreignness.

Enactments, then, are affectively and stylistically distinct objects in a world replete with objects, from which certain ones are selected as possessing a peculiar importance for us. That selectivity takes place throughout a lifetime of actions and responses which I shall clarify by identifying the four basic senses of the terms "enactment" and "to enact."

"Enactment" and "to enact" bring together strands of behavior that can be described by the four basic meanings "to enact" possesses. They are the following: (1) To enact is to set forth, to decree, to ordain. Enactments possess the properties and communal status of lasting things. (2) To enact is to inspire feelings in a person and audience, to actuate feelings, to enact dispositions. That is, enactments produce and create and establish highly cathected objects and events. (3) To enact is to represent, in the artistic sense of representation. (4) To enact is to perform in the sense best known for drama—that is, a performance.

Enactments, as social events, exhibit a number of other characteristics that will be discussed below. For example, enactments are intentional objects; they are functional wholes; they possess both cognitive and affective content and function socially in a variety of ways. Enactments emanate, in most cases, from individuals, whether they be creator or performer, or both, and make demands on those who receive them. They exist in the world of public events, and at the same time work privately, both consciously and unconsciously, in the individual. They transcend the occasion of their realization, and achieve permanence and continuity through generations of presentations. Enactments are means to social adaptation, and as such they support the efforts of the ego to achieve integration of the individual with society, and also integration of instinctual demands with rational determination of goals.

The description just given of enactments as a class of objects illustrates one of the ways in which psychoanalytic theory of art compels the philosophy of art to reconsider its conceptual systems as they have grown up in two thousand years of reflection on human making. Although the philosophical theories of the past have devoted attention to objects, the objects of our deepest cultural concern have lacked a generic name. Introduction of the term "enactment" fills that need; but more to the point here, it provides a way of talking about objects as they have been understood in the most recent of the revolutionary theories of art. Psychoanalytic theory has concentrated on cultural objects as such, distinguishing them from natural objects (some of which, of course, can and do become cultural objects), and from the domain of merely private objects that never attain participation in a tradition.

The first sense of "to enact," draws attention to a social function of enactments: they work where there is a community in being that looks back to a past and forward to accomplishments in its own established terms, and those terms include the continuous production of cultural objects. As precious and as sacred as objects created and hoarded may be, new objects must be created because of a function they perform. Treasured objects constitute wealth, to be sure, but they also make claims, assertions, and demands. However tradition-bound a set of objects may be, however much each is required to mimic its predecessor—as for example in the ancient tradition of Navajo sand painting—its *production* is an event of a cultural kind that has reasons for repetition. Thus "decree" and "ordain" both have an impersonal and a personal sense: a monarch may so act, but then, too, so may the gods, or nature itself. And in that wider sense, enactments make assertions about reality that are considered true and unchanging. The very repetitiousness of production attests to continuities in the social and natural order that the products articulate and defend. In that sense of "to enact," enactments pronounce on eternal things, things to be known and to be closely held through their representations.[6]

As anthropologists, we understand the needs described, but may think ourselves immune from or not needful of enactments in the sense just stated. The need remains; its mode of satisfaction shifts. And that is why objects we "venerate" are of a different kind from those venerated in the past: more highly individual and often intimately related to a person, such as the artist. Psychoanalytic inquiry into the life and work of artists brings us into a realm of enactments as ordinations and decrees, voices issuing from sources that we honor above the gods.

The deep feelings inspired by enactments we promote and teach. Feelings actuated by objects are some of our earliest responses to the world, and, as we shall see below, the beginning of cultural life is to be found in objects that are "transitional" in their power to carry us out of ourselves into the cultural world we grow up to participate in.[7] Early experiences of this kind have affective towardness that we as yet do not fully understand. Freud began to inquire into the relationship of early, highly cathected objects, and later object relationships in his clinical observations on fetishes and fetishism, but once again, the connection between psychosexual maturational stages and cultural life in general was not established. The significance of Freud's observations has long been recognized: our world is a world of objects cathected in a tremendously varied organizational pattern, and those patterns include objects that are parts of ourselves, of others, and representational enactments whose roles in individual lives are defined as the lives are lived.

Representation and performance are closely related though not coincident. To be a representation is not necessarily to be in need of performance, or performable. We think of paintings as nonperformable representations, and dramas as performable representations. However, in a wide metaphoric sense, all enactments are performances, for to be an enactment is to be an object that makes demands of a culturally specific kind upon participants in the tradition. If we think of performance as applying to both the performer and the witness, then my witnessing a painting is at once for me an action in which I perform—that is, I go through a specific set of responses, judgments, interpretations, and seek specific kinds of feelings. Whether an enactment is of the so-called "performing arts" or not, enactments organize and focus objects in highly cathected ways, and it is that aspect of our interaction with objects that psychoanalytic theory specifically analyzes.

Another way to look at the relationship between performance and representation is to regard performances as approximations of representations, which themselves require the infinite repetition of performance to be realized, and even then they are never fully realized. This assertion has different implications for artist and audience. For artist, a performance is an artistic act aiming at a representation, and necessarily falling short in some respect; for audience, a performance is a presentation whose limitations entail repeated witnessing.

Among Freud's followers who have attempted to broaden the psychoanalytic theory of objects, Heinz Hartmann, in *Ego Psychology and the Problem of Adaptation,* recognized the need to expand the theory of objects to meet the realities of cultural life. He quotes the philosopher John Dewey, whose theory of behavior recognizes a more inclusive setting for action than does psychoanalytic thought. "Goals, says Dewey in *Human Nature and Conduct,* are in general means to unify and to liberate present, contradictory, confused habits and drives."[8] Among the goals pursued in communal life are the creation and use of works of art, and they can be understood, in psychoanalytic terms, to realize "integrative" functions. Hartmann's point is that created objects, such as enactments, serve to integrate rational processes with the more archaic side of psychic life. He goes on to say:

The process of artistic creation is the prototype of synthetic solution, and . . . this is the most important difference between it and "fantasying." Such a tendency toward "order" is inherent in every work of art, even when its content or intent represents "disorder." This is, then, another case of "regressive adaptation": a mental achievement (whose roots are archaic) gains a new significance both for synthesis and in relation to the external world, precisely because of the detour through the archaic.[9]

Through enactments the ego achieves an integration of external and internal events; the person learns to entertain alternatives to the immediacies of experience. The ability to entertain alternatives is essential not only to ego functioning; it is as well a condition for culture. Hartmann's observation distinguishes art objects, which require a medium and ego control over creative construction, from mere fantasy. The concern of ego psychology is to draw clearly the distinction between art and fantasy, because Freud's treatment of art was sometimes ambiguous on this difference, and could be read in some places as reductive, putting art in the same class of psychic events as dream and fantasy.

Even with the elaboration upon Freud's view supplied by Hartmann, we are a long way from a satisfactory explanation of how cultural objects and events function in the community of human beings. Hartmann's emphasis on coping with the world as a function of the ego keeps the analysis on a level of organization below the social, but it does open the way to a recognition of the cognitive power of art beyond anything Freud recognized. Although it suggests the developmental side of enactments, Hartmann's observations fail to describe the stages of development, and are unaware of the need to integrate id function and ego function for the purposes of a general theory of cultural objects.

An effort to specify the developmental side of enactments, to find a path from earlier stages of object relationship to the later, cultural construction and use of objects, was attempted by D. W. Winnicott in an interesting paper that descends from his theory of "transitional objects." He distinguishes a third area of play, contrasting it with the first area of the outer actual world, and the second area of the inner psychic world. Within the third area the transitional object functions as a means to traverse the vast space between isolation and communal sharing which culminates in the cultural world.[10]

There are many suggestive thoughts in this essay, but not a really satisfactory explication. What I find useful in Winnicott's paper is the effort to relate early play with the mother, through the shared use of the transitional object, to later manifestations of work, play, and shared cultural experiences. Winnicott argues that it is in the space between mother and child—the third area—that culture begins. And he wants to separate that area from inner and outer reality. Unfortunately, this easy tripartite classification gives us trouble, and a word must be said about it simply as an epistemological analysis.

While there is reason to characterize the arena of play as Winnicott does, it ought not be contrasted with inner and outer reality in the manner he suggests. The cultural arena is part of both inner and outer reality: it is known and worked with internally, as are any psychological representations of consciousness and unconsciousness. Cultural events are accorded respect different from that of most physical events; but many cultural objects are natural objects and events, such as stones, trees, and sacred places that are distinguished by a peculiar aura of sentiment and affect. "Outer reality" can be part of the third area. Another reason to reject Winnicott's distinctions is that the interaction between child and parent, as later between various participating members of the community, draws upon both inner states and outer events to establish the space within which actions and responses to actions are forged. Winnicott's distinction between area of play, outer reality, and inner consciousness separates enactment from the sources of its representational and affective strength, for objects of play, like works of art, move in and out of the "real" world, and borrow freely from fantasy. Thus a more satisfactory way to think about transitional objects and the third area within which they function would be to encompass the entire process as one weaving together outer and inner through an object that participates in and draws upon both. It is true, I believe, that the establishment of a transitional object, and the play with and by means of it, are all preconditions for later cultural interactions. But the final achievement of cultural life relates to both inner psychic and outer physical realities in a set of ways that Winnicott's simple tripartite division cannot cope with. So let us accept the general dynamic description of the transitional object, its role in development, and let us set aside the epistemological comments as unsatisfactory.

In itself the idea of the transitional object is useful. By "transitional object" Winnicott was referring to those objects—toys, dolls, blankets, fetishistic-like things—that are the first object a child uses, and to which there is an emotional attachment. The object functions in several ways; most important, Winnicott believed, is as means to effect a transition from the symbiotic relationship with the mother to independent, self-sufficient action in the world apart from the mother. In the play process which leads developmentally to separation, and to the establishment of the distinction me–not me, the child enters a special domain in which the transitional object assumes the potential to exist as a so-and-so—that is, to exist as a character, as a part of a story endowed with a history, to possess human qualities, and to function as an affective currency in exchange between mother and child. The transitional object is highly cathected.

Mother and child participate in a drama of great complexity, at one time taking on the role of characters, at another of audience, and again as commentators. They can move in and out of the third area; the transitional object too possesses mobility, for it can "play" a variety of parts. The transitional object, in Winnicott's sense, is the first not-me object, and I am extending the description of the way the object functions well beyond his observations. Throughout the different stages of the developmental project the child learns the meaning of subject, object, character, scene, play-acting, metaphor, imaginative construction of story, and joins these possibilities to his actions. It is here that enactments begin.

All the while that the transitional object is an end of attention and love it is also a means of growth. The means of growth, I want to emphasize, is *fictional*, for the created enactment is an imaginary product that launches the child on a cultural career in which imaginary objects become real presences.

Winnicott's central idea is that the relationship between mother and child establishes a space within which culturally significant activities occur. "The place where cultural experience is located is the *potential space* between the individual and the environment (originally the object)."[11] By emphasizing "potential space" Winnicott wants to indicate that the establishment of such a space evolves over time, and through the shared activities of mother and child. Part of the process of growing up is the defining of cultural experience. From the description of play given by Winnicott, it seems that he attaches a special significance to this space, a space he refers to as the "space between," in contrast to inner awareness and the space of the external world, unbounded by parent and empty of any objects for play.

The establishment of a special place for enactments characterizes all cultural behavior of all peoples. Winnicott's suggestion that the "place" is first established between mother and child seems plausible, and that the first objects played with in that space are transitional objects also seems supported by observation. In a larger sense, cultural objects that have an enduring presence function as transitional objects, for they possess many of the essential properties of those objects: they are communal possessions, hence belong to both self and another; they allow the individual to participate in interaction with an enduring presence; they emanate an aura of protective potency; and they express externally an internal experience.

Psychoanalytic theory needs to clarify the developmental claims that are made in the theory of transitional objects, for though we assert the continuity of transitional objects from childhood play to adult cultural participation, the ways that cultural objects function are obviously far more complex and multifarious than the ways in which transitional objects function. Yet it seems to me that the very idea of transitional object is suggestive in the case of cultural objects, for they do function in a wider sense of "transitional" that will help us to expand psychoanalytic theory. The enlargement of theory I anticipate takes in two aspects of the objects we have been discussing: object as work of art, and object as complement to subject or the self. If we think of works of art as transitional objects in a metaphoric sense broader than Winnicott's, then we can ask,

To what is the metaphorical applied? "Transitional" is itself a metaphoric term, for the transitional *transfers, carries over,* moves from one domain to another domain. As metaphors carry from one domain to another, so transitional objects carry from one domain to another. They are *literally* metaphoric, if we can be allowed the seeming contradiction. *Where* they transport the participants is the interesting speculation. My suggestion is that transitional objects carry in two directions; each way is a way that passes beyond the accepted realities of inner psychic and outer physical: that is, the representational powers of transitional objects shape self-consciousnesss and the reality without. Self and object define one another through their interaction, and that interaction is mediated in part through cultural objects as transitional objects. One recent writer in the psychoanalytic tradition has stated the interrelationship as follows: "The self is defined in relation to objects and vice versa. The existence of objects guarantees the existence of the self. . . . The self changes and objects change or are succeeded by new objects, but both attachments [to self and object] persist; each is a part of the other."[12] I should like to expand this assertion, taking into account the contribution Winnicott's study of transitional objects has made to a fuller developmental theory of objects.

The implications of the assertion that self and object define one another are complex, and as yet relatively little understood, but I shall try to provide some content to the claim in the discussion of tragedy to follow (chapter 4, sections II and III). The concept of enactment under discussion here can be brought to bear on the claim that we develop as individuals in culture through the interaction with cultural objects. Enactments function as transitional objects in two directions: they refer to external reality, the sociocultural domain of tradition, and to internal reality, the developmental continuity of growing up in culture. When Winnicott claims that the transitional object is the first cultural object, he quite correctly draws our attention to a metaphoric property of the transitional object which enables it to convey the consciousness of the child from symbiotic relationship, to some degree of independence, and the first stage toward individuation. My discussion attempts to go beyond the first tentative steps, and even though the means whereby transitional objects affect the cultural disposition of the maturing individual remain hidden—to a large degree mysterious—recent work on object relations perhaps can offer a few highly speculative observations.

The clinical and theoretical contributions of Otto Kernberg have gone furthest in an attempt to amplify psychoanalytic theory in its efforts to account for the developmental interaction between persons and objects. The most basic claim Kernberg wants to make is that "the repressed unconscious, the id, is structured beyond the structural implications of primary process thinking itself."[13] This suggests the possibility that primary process thinking and the id evolve and develop in the course of a life, and that they are influenced in their organization by secondary process thought as it evolves through the empirical problems it must solve. Therefore, Kernberg speculates, the id, as well as the ego and the superego, probably changes throughout life in a way that gives the id a plasticity denied to it by Freud. The id, then, may share with the ego and the superego the developmental process which "reflects vicissitudes of the drive investment of internalized object relations and are highly structured."[14] It would follow from this that experiences with enactments, such as witnessing a tragic drama, would influence and shape the dynamic affects of unconscious process, and also would involve primary process thinking in a developing, changing set of object relationships over the course of a life. The possibility that primary process thinking is affected by secondary process thinking enlarges Freud's beliefs about primary process thought with an enduring developmental growth, and has interesting implications for a theory of enactments. Because of their powerful affective properties, and because of their representation of deep developmental conflicts, enactments establish a set of objects to which a lifelong accommodation and adjustment are required. The unconscious beliefs, attitudes, values that are private and those that are shared undergo affirmation and reorganization with repeated encounters.

Kernberg's observations would apply to transitional objects at every stage of development; yet the assumed influence of object relations upon id structures leaves unexplained, as indeed Freud's speculations on art left unexplained, the ways in which enactments influence psychic development. All that can be said at this time is that there are clinical observations that tend to strengthen a hypothesis about primary process thought that was often entertained: "There is an intimate relation between conscious and unconscious elements throughout the entire sequence of intrapsychic development."[15] And further, there is a causal claim: "The light of consciousness not only illuminates the derivatives of the unconscious, but also contributes to shaping them."[16] If it is true that object relations enter into every level of psychic life, then a developmental theory of objects, such as the theory of enactments, would have to consider the psychological dimension of object relations where cultural objects are concerned as basic to any philosophy of art. And, indeed, there does seem to be a developmental trajectory in the history of our involvement with enactments, not only in the history of criticism as such, but in the history of the philosophy of art. Depth and complexity of enactments is not simply a function of historical context, but is also, we may conjecture, a manifestation of deep unconscious responses to the objects that constitute a tradition. Investigation of the history of enactments in this respect awaits both theoretical and empirical advances.

The theory of enactments is presented in order to carry the developmental process of the cultural use of objects through to the adult stages. In general, art history has recognized these stages far more adequately in cultural terms than has psychoanalytic theory. In the hands of the art historian Adrian Stokes, deeply influenced by psychoanalytic thought, we find a description of object relationships that recognizes the way art history and developmental theory of objects can describe the complexity of enactments and our use of them in maturity:

Our relationship to all objects seems to me to be describable in terms of two extreme forms, the one a very strong identification with the object, whether projective or introjective, whereby a barrier between self and not-self is undone, the other a commerce with a self-sufficient and independent object at arm's length. In all times except the earliest weeks of life, both of these relationships, in vastly different amalgams, are in play together, as is shown not only by psychoanalysis but by art, since the work of art is *par excellence* a self-sufficient object as well as a configuration that we absorb or to which we lend ourselves as manipulators. (The first generic difference between styles lies in the varying combinations by which these two extremes are conveyed to us.) Here is to be observed a fundamental connection of art with the culture from which it arises; for, art helps us both to identify ourselves with some aspect of our culture, to incorporate cultural activities or to reject them, and at the same time to contemplate them as if they were fixed and hardy objects. From the angle of contemplation culture *is* art—hence, once more, the necessity of having art—since culture is most easily seen as an object for contemplation in aesthetic terms.[17]

Stokes draws attention to the dynamic play between the individual consciousness and the objects of culture. His description could be read as the mature phase of object relations which at some later point is achieved, following the initial phase described by Winnicott. Stokes attends to the identification–objectification distinction as it occurs in our commerce with enactments. But he does not stress the transitional function of objects which follows from the duality of identification–objectification. That an object can be a transitional object follows from the twin relationships Stokes points to: there are those special objects, enactments in the vocabulary used here, to which we have a relationship at once identifying with and separating from. And that relationship has close affinities to the relationship of child to parent in the description of the third area offered by Winnicott. We are here, as so often in psychoanalytic writings, dealing with descriptions using different terminologies yet approaching similar kinds of events and interpreting them in the light of a theory held in common. But differences of vocabulary make comparisons difficult and perhaps suspect.

Despite that necessary caution in making comparisons, I see continuity between Winnicott, Kernberg, and Stokes. In each case, though there is continuity from one to another, there is also a lack. The lack comes in where we need to understand how transition occurs, how objects of the special sort—enactments—function in our later life in realizing the metaphorical translation from immediate private consciousness to culture. Stokes puts his finger on the duality of these objects: "The work of art is *par excellence* a self-sufficient object as well as a configuration that we absorb or to which we lend ourselves as manipulators," but he fails to take the next step in the analysis. Perhaps the very difficulty of describing the condition of object relations on the cultural level inhibits the effort. I find that the best descriptions here turn to philosophical language and are sometimes embedded in literary objects. A philosophical attempt to move the analysis to the level of cultural experience has been made by the French philosopher Maurice Merleau-Ponty, who attaches to it the rather grandiose phrase "metaphysical consciousness." I would prefer to think of the condition as one of "cultural consciousness."

From the moment I recognize that my experience, precisely insofar as it is my own, makes me accessible to what is not myself, that I am sensitive to the world and to others, all the beings which objective thought placed at a distance draw singularly near to me. Or, conversely, I recognize my affinity with them; I am nothing but an ability to echo them, to understand them. My life seems absolutely individual and absolutely universal to me. This recognition of an individual life which animates all past and contemporary lives and receives its entire life from them, of a light which flashes from them to us contrary to all hope—this is metaphysical consciousness, whose first stage is surprise at discovering the confrontation of opposites and whose second stage is recognition of their identity in the simplicity of *doing*. Metaphysical consciousness has no other objects than those of experience: this world, other people, human history, truth, culture.[18]

Merleau-Ponty's "metaphysical consciousness" warns us that the psychoanalytic description of object relations lacks a sufficiently defined cultural dimension. I have attempted to introduce this dimension, and to demonstrate that in its own terms psychoanalytic theory can include the cultural. *Totem and Taboo* and *Moses and Monotheism,* when given their philosophical reading, provide a framework for a theory of enactments. The work of ego psychology, of child analysis in Winnicott's terms, and the work of object relations theory all help to widen the scope of a psychoanalytic theory of art. From the investigations made by psychiatrists who, like Freud, kept close to the clinical base, we can advance psychoanalytic theory of art to the mature stages of development. Freud's early speculations provided a crude cultural profile, seeing later stages of psychic life as inevitable outcomes of earlier; but Freud did not attend to the details of the complex ways individuals and cultural objects interact to establish a tradition. The greater attention given to objects by the work of Winnicott on transitional objects, of Kernberg on object relations, and of Stokes on works of art, amplifies and complements the schematic early speculations of Freud. We are therefore in a better position to establish a psychoanalytic theory of culture that will address itself to the properties of cultural objects as works of art and the way those properties themselves participate in the lifelong mastery of culture.

III So far, I have argued that enactments amplify and complete the psychoanalytic theory of objects. In addition, enactments themselves are cultural events that represent and in some cases analyze the cultural conflicts characterizing cultures. The expanded form of a psychoanalytic theory of culture proposed here implies that through enactments members of a culture might gain the self-consciousness to enable them to cope with cultural conflicts more successfully. However, this way of looking at enactments, implying that they themselves may be means to resolution, as well as representations, of conflict, seems to me problematical.

Freud's belief that there no longer may be such mechanisms reflects his own pessimism and his immersion in the present condition we call "modernity." Indeed, it may be that one of the conditions of modernity is the loss of a tradition of enactments, and that to regain whatever coherence there might once have been, and to avoid the cultural disintegration Freud feared was upon us, we must reestablish enactments as culturally significant events. Without that, the psychological health of modern society cannot be good. But whether or not it was good in the past is a question we shall forever dispute and never be able to answer.

Traditionally, in Freud's writings, the psychoanalytic theory of objects was treated as a function of the theory of instincts. Instinctual life was defined in terms of the objects toward which instincts are directed. When psychoanalytic theory attempted to analyze cultural objects, they were treated as highly cathected objects within the orbit of individual affects. However, for the artist, and the audience, cultural objects achieve, and usually sustain, a public life that puts them into a much larger context than that of individual psychodynamics. Hence a psychoanalytic theory of cultural objects is required to consider psychologically important objects that exist in a tradition from the point of view of the ego. The public, shared, communal existence of cultural objects—the domain of ego functioning—

has more often called upon sociology and anthropology than upon psychoanalytic theory. Yet the ways cultural objects work for us is psychological in a basic respect—i.e., they are part of the maturational process in which individuals grow up and take their place in a cultural tradition in large part through interaction with cultural objects. A developmental theory then must also be called upon in dealing with works of art, but it must be expanded in the ways discussed above.

Growing up has two dimensions describable in psychoanalytic terms: the first, development through the psychosexual stages from infancy into adulthood which can best be described in terms of the family; the second, developmental stages in cultural internalization and externalization which can best be described in terms of a transaction between persons and objects, especially enactments. The stages of cultural life can be crudely described in the following four stages.

1. The first stage is marked by the externalization of objects, giving them a separate, yet deeply narcissistic existence, as described by Winnicott. The first steps toward the externalization and attribution of separate existence to objects seem to occur between mother and child in a kind of fantasy play. Yet through shared fantasy the world begins to exist outside the merely private interests of the child. Regularities of nature become integrated into expectations and beliefs, but at this stage events are interpreted as expressing dynamic properties of love, hate, compliance, indifference, and hostility. Externalization begins through a narcissistic identification under the command of need and wish. Need and wish create objects, and endow objects with meaning. Primary narcissism lays the foundation for the culturally mature condition we might think of as "group narcissism," which emerges as the individual reaches later stages of internalization of enactments. Shared identifications characterize a people who possess a tradition; through the tradition, enactments are recognized to possess wisdom, artistic excel-

lence, continuity of style, and to serve as a source for the continued making of objects in the tradition.

2. The second stage, in which moral discriminations begin, is maturationally joined to the first separation stage and grows alongside of it. The moral stage sees the internalization of rules, precepts, admonitions, and the use of cultural objects in the reinforcement of superego identity. Enactments enter here with great force, for they deal with many of the maturational problems of the moral life. In one of Freud's essays, written when he was surveying the complexities of object relations, there is a passage that describes the role of enactments in focusing developmental issues.

The course of childhood development leads to an ever-increasing detachment from parents, and their personal significance for the superego recedes into the background. To the images they leave behind there are then linked the influences of teachers and authorities, self-chosen models and publicly recognized heroes, whose figures need no longer be introjected by an ego which has become more resistant. The last figure in the series that began with the parents is the dark power of Destiny which only the fewest of us are able to look upon as impersonal.[19]

Our moral sensibilities respond to enactments, as they provide many of the models to which Freud's essay refers. Enactments further this side of the moral life not only by their representations but also by the cultural conditions under which they are witnessed, shared, and learned, for communal participation is essential to enactments.

At this stage strong transference relationships exist between person and object, for each side of the representation and response mirrors the other. The object realizes itself in the consciousness of the receiver, and the receiver witnesses consciousness in the object. As in the relationship between analyst and patient, for which the concept of transference was developed, enactment and audience direct affect back and forth. That reflection is taken up again and again in the tradition which comments and re-reflects upon the relationship. The tendency at this stage is for deep internalization of cultural norms and the projection into enactments of the representation of the individual who receives them. Freud's reference to "the dark power of Destiny" recognizes the intimate relationship that exists between the individual and the object as they contemplate the inevitability of death.[20]

3. The third, aesthetic, stage liberates us from deep internalization with a re-externalization of the objects which now exist independently as objects in a tradition. These objects are to be mastered through the adaptive processes of growing up. The process of mastery goes on through life, for enactments need to be reconsidered with every change in historical perspective and with the introduction of new theories. The interdependence of enactment and theory now becomes clear. It is at this stage that the philosophy of art and art itself are recognized to be functions of one another. And this is, therefore, the stage of *manifestoes*. In one respect our whole tradition is a series of manifestoes in which enactments undergo interpretative reorganization. Respect for theory, as well as respect for cultural objects, puts the person in a position to join private recollection with public recognition in the cultural condition I have referred to as a shared tradition.

4. Thus the fourth stage of re-internalization of cultural reality comes about. Enactments establish themselves as a reality to be known, as permanent and as valuable as the events of the physical world. Memory preserves performances, and in the case of extraordinary gifts enables creative addition to cultural objects to be made. The addition builds upon *style* as it has been defined through the tradition. The final stage of internalization endows style with its flexibility to be both a traditional structure and a creative instrument whose variables can now be tested for new sets of values.

Identification with style in its traditional forms, and the exploitation of traditional styles in new formal structures, is believed by many anthropologists to be a condition necessary to culture, a condition of cultural communication. Evidence for this hypothesis has been most systematically sought in the French school of anthropology (Durkheim, Mauss, Lévi-Strauss) and there remains dispute over just what sorts of things are communicated through recognitions of stylistic constancy. But the point is suggestive, even while undergoing revision: that human beings objectify their beliefs and values through enactments. This claim appears more obvious on the level of character and action, the sorts of events psychoanalytic theory addresses, than on the level of intimate stylistic repetitions; yet at both levels there is a distinction to be made that has to do with the nature of enactments themselves as communicating media. Enactments do communicate values, attitudes, beliefs, ways of seeing nature and art, and a great many other "messages." Their power to communicate such a variety of contents is due to their representational complexity: they represent the world and the cultural tradition; they also represent the subjectivity of the maker, the individual known through the privacy of events that are expressed only within and through enactments. In addition, enactments are *self-referential*: they refer to their representational powers toward the world, so they also refer to their representational powers toward the privacy of the reality to be known only in the object itself. Anthropological theories of cultural communication neglect the privacy of enactments, their hiddenness and their subjectivity. Psychoanalytic theory sees the self-referential aspects of enactments because it has a concern for both sides of the process of communication: the need to communicate, the need to preserve privacy; but its limitation brings it back again and again to its preoccupation with the hidden. The effort to expand the theory through the concept of enactments makes demands upon it that will, I hope, force its future formulations to a more fruitful consideration of cultural phenomena. In this respect we have benefited from the recent clinical work of psychoanalysts such as D. W. Winnicott, who was very sensitive to the limitations of the classical theory. He wrote:

Although healthy persons communicate and enjoy communicating, the other fact is equally true, that *each individual is an isolate, permanently non-communicating, permanently unknown, in fact unfound.*

In life and in living this hard fact is softened by the sharing that belongs to a whole range of cultural experience. At the centre of each person is an incommunicado element, and this is sacred and most worthy of preservation.[21]

Winnicott goes on to develop this idea from evidence gathered in psychoanalytic treatment. He points out that communication is of many kinds: it can be explicit, it can be silent, it can be intermediate between the silent and the explicit. The intermediate mode uses concealment and occasional, dramatic, revelation in the process of revealing the self. This mode of communication is also frequently used in the communication of enactments.

Winnicott observed the need to preserve privacy in work with children, and went on to study the various modes of communication and non-communication which the cultural tradition fostered. Each cultural tradition has its own way to protect the areas of hiddenness that Winnicott refers to as "non-communicating" from violation, but every person growing up experiences the demands for exposure and publicity which places the "sacred" part of the self in jeopardy. The risk of being exposed to forced disclosure itself becomes part of the ground for the creation of enactments, since they subtly represent delicate matters requiring hiddenness, and are able to disclose the otherwise inexpressible. Enactments are themselves both communicating and non-communicating objects.

The complexity of cultural objects in this respect was one of the conditions that led some of Freud's followers to attempt a reformulation, with greater attention to the work of the ego, of those ways of coping with objects that Freud dealt with through excessive attention to the primary process of the id. The capacity of the ego to make use of primary process thinking has been one of the concerns of the so called ego psychology developed by thinkers close to Freud. It is through the ego that shared cultural objects and shared cultural assessments come into the lives of individuals.

IV The process of accommodation to and mastery of the cultural tradition has been treated under the part of psychoanalytic theory called "ego psychology," because the ego is that function of psychic life in which cognitive and adaptive processes go on. The ego also has been considered that part of psychic life in which the instinctual force finds cognitive enforcement and direction toward constructive work. In the phrase used by Anna Freud, maturation strives to achieve an "intellectualization of instinctual life." This implies a making over of instinctual object relations into conscious integration of objects into the life of the individual. That cannot be realized without the creation of representational objects such as works of art. Without enactment, intellectualization of instinctual life is impossible.

Anna Freud writes:

This intellectualization of instinctual life, the attempt to lay hold on the instinctual processes by connecting them with ideas which can be dealt with in consciousness, is one of the most general, earliest and most necessary acquirements of the human ego.[22]

By "intellectualization of instinctual life" Anna Freud is referring to several processes: the process of maturation in general, whose aim is mastery of instinctual impulses; the process of strengthening the ego through relating ideas and feelings; and the process of expanding consciousness so that instinctual energies can be constructively used in the creation of objects.

One of the most important constructive uses of instinct is that which culminates in enactments. In this process both nature and culture are rendered *for me* by means of objects whose representations are themselves representations of the intellectualization of instinctual life. For enactments represent not only events—as in telling a story—they also present objects themselves as structured by the forces of creative making. The intellectualization of instinctual life expresses itself in *style*.

Supplementary to Anna Freud's developmental account, that of Heinz Hartmann treats the instinctual and intellectual as developing together out of an at-first-undifferentiated set of organismic activities. Very early on—from the beginning of there being object relations at all—the intellectualization of the instinctual occurs. Thus with Winnicott's description of the third area, and the force of play in cultural life, we can see that play and ego develop together. This is the point of Hartmann's analysis in *Ego Psychology and the Problem of Adaptation:*

The inner world and its functions make possible an adaptation process which consists of two steps: withdrawal from the external world and return to it with improved mastery. The fact that goals are not directly approached but reached by interpolated detours (means) is a decisive step in evolution.[23]

Withdrawal and return requires all of the cultural means that have evolved through thousands of years of human communal life; and of those cultural means, enactments are most crucial because they compel individuals to participate in the experiences of the tradition. We are content, as a rule, to think of the tradition as the monuments to be met, desired, and prized. But their contribution to our lives lies in more than gratitude for beauty and wisdom. They shape us, as they were shaped. Hartmann's emphasis on adaptation states the integration this way:

It is crucial for the ego that it can use regulations, while it simultaneously takes into account the irrationality of other mental achievements. The rational plan must include the irrational as a fact. . . . Anthropomorphic and irrational thought can be fruitful even in the realm of scientific thinking; conversely, the need for rationality can be a symptom or a defense, etc., in pathological cases. . . . Even cursory reflection will show that the foundations of psychoanalysis as a therapeutic procedure indeed imply this relationship between regard for the rational and regard for the irrational elements.[24]

Enactments are the cultural means we have to combine the rational and irrational achievements of psychic life, for they take as one of their central concerns the struggle over integration. And they are endowed, by their place in culture, with the power to focus the exchange of strong affects in the relationship of transference. The mastery thus achieved relies in part on the process Hartmann calls "regressive adaptation," by which he means that "a mental achievement (whose roots are archaic) gains a new significance both for synthesis and in relation to the external world, precisely because of the detour through the archaic."[25]

Hartmann's observations can be amplified in terms of the present discussion. The process of making which calls upon primary process thinking (that is what is meant by "detour through the archaic") is expressed and exhibited in the objects themselves. The history of cultural objects, especially the history of art, could be written in terms of the artistic and aesthetic means to this end. Indeed, a psychoanalytically oriented art history would attempt, in the manner of Hartmann's speculations, to push the theory of interpretation out beyond the limited boundaries observed in early psychoanalytic writings. With the notion of "adaptive process" Hartmann is beginning that elaboration, suggesting that the history of culture is in part a story that explains how mastery of primary process thinking took place. It occurred, in part, through the creation of those objects I have called "enactments," and there are benefits to increasing self-consciousness in the adaptive process. Heightened self-consciousness and more intense insight into human action follows from the close study of enactments themselves.

There is an interesting, perhaps theoretically significant,

complementarity between Hartmann and Kernberg on this point—that is, on the ways in which primary process and secondary process thinking interact. Kernberg argues (see above, p. 64) that secondary process thinking has an effect upon primary process thought which we must think of developmentally, contrary to the view Freud held that primary process thought was laid down early and did not develop through the maturational life process. Hartmann sees the process of "regressive adaptation" as one in which secondary process thought is influenced by the capacity of the person dealing with objects to draw upon primary process thinking. In sum, the complementary additions to ego psychology suggest that the developmental project in the lifelong commerce with objects is far more complex than psychoanalytic theory originally recognized. Yet even with the additions of Hartmann and Kernberg, an aspect of enactments is neglected, the aspect that enables them to be the meeting ground for the interaction of primary and secondary process thought: that is the property of *style*. Style is an ego-controlled organizing structure with roots deep in the unconscious, and it is through style that enactments are able to establish a tradition whose highly cathected objects are at once possessed—they are "mine"—and are expressive—they are manifestations of subjectivity—existing in the world as objects for others to experience with their private histories of subjectivity.

V Style is the structure peculiar to enactments and insofar as enactments possess person-like qualities, it is in their style that they achieve this property. We attribute intentions to persons; we attribute style to cultural objects. As made things, carrying the mark of tradition and maker, cultural objects exhibit their intentions through their styles. This is to argue on a kind of analogy, that objects possess person-like qualities in terms of properties peculiar to them—that is, styles—and that these properties are perceived and responded to, as intentional acts of persons are perceived and responded to. In arguing this way, I include both the structural and the motivational senses of "intention," with the conscious and unconscious aspects part of the definition. Thus to say, "Style is the intention of enactments," implies that stylistically, as well as thematically, enactments will possess a conscious and an unconscious aspect, and will be responded to with both conscious and unconscious affects, beliefs, and attitudes.

Freud maintained that the consistency of enactments was to be found in their thematic material: that certain psychosexual themes appeared again and again. And as we have seen, behind that assertion lay the assumption of a specific kind of psychological purposiveness, the purpose of a need to fulfill a wish. It was relatively easy in our discussion, once the psychoanalytic theory of dreams was worked out, to apply the distinction manifest–latent to enactments. But the discussion of art in Freud's theoretical writings left undeveloped the manifest–latent distinction, and explicitly left out the complex organizing principle of style.

My contention here is that the constancy of enactments derives as much, or more, from their style as it does from the common thematic material identified by psychoanalytic theory. But the idea of style has to be understood as a functional whole with a structure that sustains a constant effect. The intention of the object is to sustain the effect through the style. The object itself is perceived and responded to as an object with an intention, possessing some of the characteristics of a person because of its expressive content and its purposive organization.

Each theory of art lays down a character analysis, claiming to lay bare the *real* intention of the object. But, as we regard the history of manifestoes, we come to see that each of them provides at best a limited interpretation—"limited," that is, because the definition of intention reflects a choice. Choosing expresses unconscious and historically traditional ways to establish a boundary within which interpretation takes place. In the case of psychoanalytic interpretation—and here as elsewhere the theory is the ideology—a wide range of unspecified variables is simply left out of account. In this, psychoanalytic theory is like every other theory; but because all theories are this way, it must be understood that any one theory is necessarily incomplete. That is, each interpretation draws a boundary around the variables that can be considered in making an interpretation; the boundary is in fact part of the interpretation. Hence the intention of the object where the object is an enactment is a function of the style and of the manifesto as they are both expressed by the object and understood by the people who use the object.

This way of analyzing "intention" puts the psychoanalytic interpretation in a larger theoretical setting which then admits competing and complementary methods of interpretation. Since the intention of a cultural object, such as a work of art, is ideologically influenced and historically conditioned, a history of interpretation is a necessary part of the history of art. In such a history, the psychoanalytic is an interpretative method, and also a theory with an intention of its own like that of the cultural objects it interprets.

One conclusion of my proposed extension of psychoanalytic theory is that the concept of intention allows us to treat objects in a defined context, but denies us the comfort of ideological interpretations as fixed or demonstrable. There is no "correct" interpretation if by this we mean an interpretation of the object that would *exclude* all other interpretations. However, on whatever theory the interpretation is carried out, the intention of the object reveals two orders of reference: one is a reference to realities already partially known in nature and in culture, yet realities that are further explored in the individual enactment. The other is a reference to unconscious assumptions and dispositions that are externalized in the object in the same way that latent dream thoughts are in the manifest content of the dream. They are "in" the object as iconographical elements of structure to which we respond by feelings and by thoughts.

When we experience feelings and thoughts in the presence of cultural objects, we explore our own unconscious beliefs and dispositions as they are externalized and identified; but to say they are "identified" does not mean they are consciously entertained, for what is identified can be unconscious as well as conscious. Thoughts provoked by enactments are valued without necessarily being translatable into specific ideologies. Thus ideologies are not the intentions of cultural objects; but ideologies may become the "believed in" meanings of enactments, and this happens again and again in the histories and vicissitudes of objects.

As the residues of celebration, as the vessels of belief, and as the fastenings for tradition, enactments have become the only objects our culture recognizes as constituting a tradition; the wisdom of these creations may be the last kind of sustained deliverance we possess. That they have become the sole objects of inquiry in the humanistic disciplines seems evident. How they can then be a shaping force in science and the technical professions we are attempting to determine. That is the central task of our culture now. And it appears at times trivializing, for enactments have become widely abused, questioned, and misunderstood. How shall we get back to a common sense of their energies and gratifications? I have proposed one way to attempt that, with a philosophy of art that takes its developmental structure from psychoanalytic theory. Celebrating as it does the inheritance of enactments, it proposes the commitment to an external world of culture in which we dwell. The exploration of that realm need never end, for the searcher is compelled to create as well as study the objects sought.

In the following chapters, explorations of concepts, and concentrated study of individual objects, will be undertaken in terms of psychoanalytic theory.

IV

Psychoanalytic Theory at Work: Style, Expression, Truth

I Psychoanalytic approaches to art generate their own interesting interpretations, and as well a variety of objections; a good way to see psychoanalytic theory at work is to read an analysis by a responsible critic, and to consider as well the objections with which those of a specifically historical orientation respond. The following accounts are aimed at understanding the work of the Austrian sculptor Messerschmidt, and come from the work of the art historian-psychoanalyst Ernst Kris and the art historians Rudolf and Margot Wittkower.[1]

Kris begins his interpretation of the busts by Messerschmidt with the observation that change occurs in his style when he turns from court sculpture to physiognomic studies of heads. "This shift of interest," Kris writes, "is motivated by several factors, some of which are directly linked to his mental illness and to the specific content of his delusions." The causal analysis Kris offers rests upon psychological rather than political or strictly stylistic-historical grounds.

Kris continues his analysis by turning to the stylistic problems raised by the change in sculptural presentation: "Human expressions are turned into grimaces serving magic functions, which could in outline be interpreted." They are then interpreted first artistically, then psychologically. On the artistic level Kris points out that on a second level of artistic activity, as it were, the artist has endeavored to conceal the magic meaning of his grimaces by external attributes, such as changing coiffures or generally coloring the facial constellation with some expressive elements. An attempt is made to justify the largest possible number of those elements, which were prescribed by the delusional thoughts and the magic function. Thus he strived to endow with a meaning understandable to his public (but secondary) what was originally meaningful only to himself and was part of his delusional thinking.

And on a psychological level, Kris argues,

May we not assume that private or "secret" meanings are attached to all or many elements of the artist's work, and particularly to the formal elements for which he shows preference in one way or another? Favorable circumstances provide us in the case of Messerschmidt, a psychotic individual, with data which throw some light on this problem. We are enabled, at least in a crude and approximate fashion, to distinguish those elements in the treatment of his medium which are determined by his individual psychological predispositions (in this case by his delusion) from others which are generally intelligible without recourse to such an individual frame of reference and could therefore be generally effective. Individual and "private" meanings of this kind are obviously an integral part also of the structure of the works of normal artists. In the ideal case these meanings cannot be separated from the whole of the structure; presumably all details and traits are socially meaningful. It seems reasonable to assume that the manner in which "the private meanings" are integrated into the structure of the artistic product is of decisive importance for the nature (and perhaps the "value") of the artistic creation.

Kris' method of analyzing the busts of the sculptor Messerschmidt has its origin in the interpretative techniques Freud sketched in his discussions of works of art. We see how much further the sketch has been filled in, and how much more Kris is able to bring into his analysis than earlier practitioners of psychoanalytic interpretation could bring to bear on a single subject. The reason for Kris' greater penetration and sophistication is his training as an art historian, as well as his having benefited from the development of ego psychology, which he helped to shape with Hartmann and Loewenstein. This development in psychoanalytic theory emphasized the role of the ego, the ways in which the human organism adapted itself to the environment, and the importance in maturational explanation of conscious thought.

At the same time, Kris' description of the Messerschmidt pieces draws attention to the way in which the pure plastic structures of the face function for the artist and for the beholder. Kris here relies upon his art-historical training to bring into our awareness what I have come to refer to as the "iconography of the medium." Just as specific objects in painting and sculpture can be interpreted iconographically, so the very formal elements of art have a meaning in terms of immediate perception and immediate affect.[2] Psychoanalytic sensitivity to the medium as a symbolic form is an extension of the observations devoted to least discriminable elements of gesture, speech, expression, and physical stance. Taking advantage of the interpretations which arise in clinical analysis, Kris draws attention to the seemingly unimportant expressive features of the Messerschmidt busts. In doing this, Kris extends the interpretative method of psychoanalytic theory to the nonrepresentational parts of sculpture.

The objections to Kris' conclusions stated by the Wittkowers are not concerned with the treatment of the medium as such, but are directed to the psychological assessment of Messerschmidt. They argue that an artist's oeuvre can readily contain both official and private works without requiring a psychological model of explanation. They point out that "the practice [of creating both public and private works] appeared as early as the sixteenth century, became more and more common and marked, for instance in the work of Goya, Messerschmidt's great contemporary. Nor is it a sign of insanity that Messerschmidt endowed his 'private' works with private meaning."[3]

One obvious reply to this argument is that the same kinds of conclusions might be reached regarding Goya as regarding

Messerschmidt. But putting that aside—and all the problems a general thesis of artists' personalities raises—it should be pointed out that arguing from historical continuities and shared artistic purposes yet does not refute Kris' interpretation. Not only is Messerschmidt's work unusually riven, but we have accounts of his fantasy system that suggest the private meanings overwhelm the public forms. We *see* in his work something bizarre; and however much we are puzzled by the work of, say, Goya, we do not have the same kind of response to the paintings. Furthermore, however the historical evidence falls out, there are always psychological grounds of explanation whose relevance has to be determined in each case. We have to be guided in our evaluation and interpretation by our responses to the object. It is precisely in regard to this domain of sensitivity to responses, of the developed capacity to be analytical about affects and associations, that psychoanalytic knowledge is really essential. Common stylistic and thematic repetitions of an age do not fully account for felt responses, nor do they explain the individuality of thoughts and associations entertained when close attention is paid to the object.

The Wittkowers argue that the "secret meanings" would remain just that; yet Kris is attempting, in moving to the fantasy system of the artist, to build upon a basic discovery of clinical observation. The seemingly secret and obscure may, upon the use of the right method, turn out to be available and artistically meaningful. This hunch, which Kris attempted to confirm in his inquiry, draws a parallel between the means psychoanalysis employs to understand psychotic behavior and the means the art historian employs to understand unusual events in the domain of art.

It was observed by Freud that in certain psychotic states images function like words, and there is a confusion on the part of the psychotic person between things and words. Thus he argued that things which are represented imagistically in the unconscious can, in some extreme psychotic states, come to replace the words of consciousness, and begin to function as a language. Images represent ideas, instead of words representing ideas, and the result is primary process thinking expressed in the conscious by a "language" of images, rather than a language of words. Freud's clinical observations in this area of psychotic behavior are too limited to be of general theoretical explanation, but he pointed out a distortion of thinking that takes things to be ideational in a linguistic sense, and that translates syntactic relationships in language into physical forces that the sick person believes coerce behavior.[4]

Freud's observations on psychotic states, because they are based on limited experience with the most extreme conditions of thought distortion, both contribute to the interpretation Kris wants to make of the Messerschmidt busts and at the same time introduce difficulties for us. Kris is attempting to apply an observation of Freud's to art: "A single word can come to represent a whole train of thought," Freud wrote in the essay "The Unconscious." This is correct, and does have application to the metaphoric function of both words and images in the arts. However, it fails to distinguish two ways in which symbols function: the way they function for somebody who is psychotic, as Messerschmidt was, and for somebody who is the normal observer of the art that may be produced under psychotic states. For Messerschmidt, the details of the busts he produced may well have been *real* in the same sense that they were for him both more representational than they are for us, and less representational than they are for us. To Messerschmidt the busts may have been real presences; to us, since we stand outside his fantasy system, they are distinctively structured objects with a style that we respond to with complex feelings. It is the experience of the observer that psychoanalytic theory must help to explain without exclusive recourse to the possibly psychotic artist on the one side, and without total dependence upon the history of art on the other. Thus I seek a psychoanalytic interpretation *of the object,* not of the artist.

Yet the relationship between artist and object must be conceptualized within the framework established by psychoanalytic
theory. In my earlier discussion of transference and countertransference (see above, chapter 2, section II), I argued that
those concepts could be extended beyond the clinical use to
which they had been traditionally put. In the following discussion I shall continue to expand the senses of those terms, and
the ways in which they may be applied to artist, object, and
audience.

By "countertransference" I refer to the response of the viewer
to the peculiarities of the object in terms of associations and
interpretations that the viewer's unconscious thought provides.
Countertransference itself is metaphorically extended in its
application to the Messerschmidt case, for ordinarily we use
the word with its co-determined term "transference." Their
usage in the clinical situation presupposes an ongoing exchange between patient and analyst through which a verification procedure emerges. For in the clinical exchange there are
associations on both sides, new evidence brought forward from
the past that tends to discard some hypotheses of interpretation, and to strengthen others. In the case of works of art the
concept countertransference is more difficult to apply, and yet
I think it is relevant. The problem its introduction poses is this:
how do we know that the responses we have to an object like
the Messerschmidt busts is one that can claim some objective
status in the world of shared responses, and that the responses
are not simply private and idiosyncratic?

It is at this point that the view of the Wittkowers must inter-
vene, for, it could be argued, verification depends on art-historical criteria, such as common themes, shared styles, evidence
from documents, and the like. The deficiency of the Wittkowers' art-historical approach is precisely in the realm of strong
affect, the kinds of feelings we have with works of art that are
immediate responses to the objects and that no amount of historical reference can explain. To point out that other artists had

a double creative life does not explain the peculiarities of the Messerschmidt busts, any more than it allows us to understand the more extreme art of a painter like Goya. We seek a meaning in the objects under consideration, a meaning or set of feelings that we can share, starting from the privacy of our individual responses, and moving to explication of the objects in their uniqueness.

To achieve an appreciation of the objects' uniqueness, we must bring together the art-historical and the psychoanalytic, for which most members of an audience will not have the requisite information and skill; yet they will respond to the unconscious material. If the psychoanalytic interpreter is to move beyond unconscious responses to unconscious material, he must raise his response into consciousness—that is, find a language in which he can *explain* the meaning.

This is a sense of the term "explain" different from the usual mode of interpretation that constituted the method developed by Freud. Freud worked on the level of large iconographic representations; in contrast, Kris, the art historian, takes the most basic formal structures of the art and attempts to interpret them. Of course, Kris can do that in part because of the movement of modern art which denies the importance of "content" in the sense assumed by Freud. For example, the sculptor Boccioni, as if issuing a manifesto for the kind of interpretation Kris offers, defended the purpose of modern material art this way: in all the arts "the traditionally exalted place of subject matter" must be "abolished; . . . sculpture cannot make its goal the episodic reconstruction of reality."[5] The insistence on abstract formalism in modern sculpture is a conscious insistence on a universally fundamental sculptural value that has always played a part in material art. In this respect, the kinds of iconographic elements studied by the psychoanalytic art historian are fundamental to all and every "reading" of a work, not just to works of the sort Boccioni created. Identification of the expressive forms which constitute the iconography of the medium is essential to all interpretations. Hence the psychoanalytic reading of the Messerschmidt busts has implications for all the work carried out in art history. Kris' contribution refines method and enlarges sensibility. Hence, it seems to me, the strictures formulated by the Wittkowers do more than miss the point of Kris' contribution; they also fail to discern an avenue of study that will become increasingly important to art history as it concentrates attention on the formal properties of the immediately perceived. One way to account for that necessary narrowing of attention is to place upon the art historian an obligation to share the aesthetic concerns of the artist as artist. Art history must think not only of continuities and shared values, but also of privacies and the attendant idiosyncratic values, with, finally, the artistic necessity to strike out in new directions. The psychoanalytic interpretation of art attempts to bring up for art-historical attention unique as well as common elements in the objects to be interpreted. In that sense, psychoanalytic approaches to art do more than simply interpret in the manner of the theory; they provide material for other theories to account for. This point has been made in a somewhat different way, but one relevant to the discussion here, by Norman Holland: "A psychoanalytic reading of a literary work in terms of fantasy also has a special status. It is not simply a reading parallel to other readings from ideologies, Marxist, Swedenborgian, Christian humanist, or whatever; it is the material from which other such readings are made."[6]

The fantasy system of an artist, such as the system discovered and interpreted by Kris, when it becomes a motive to artistic creativity on the part of the artist who is truly an artist, seizes the structures of artistic organization—be they words, visual shapes, colors, harmonic relationships—and endows them with *aesthetic* properties. It is to the apprehension of the aesthetic that the beholder's response is initially directed. In that initial encounter, psychoanalytic observations well understand that "the aesthetic" includes far more than formal properties alone; it includes most especially those immediate expressive qualities of feeling to which countertransference is an inevitable response of the audience. The artist, creating the object in the cultural tradition of inherited objects, endows his work with all the transference he unconsciously expresses. And the audience responds with all the countertransference it experiences, on both a conscious and an unconscious level.

The transference of the artist obviously cannot be toward the beholder in the same sense that it is manifested in the response to the tradition, yet the artist anticipates the audience in ways that do shape the transference, and to that extent there is a countertransference to a transference that in metaphoric ways represents the audience. Hence in the busts of Messerschmidt what we see is not only the private fantasy system but an artistic system that the fantasy has taken hold of and invested with values drawn in part from the fantasy system. Artistic making as an activity stands in the tradition the artist inherits and knows, a tradition that refers to an audience as well as to other objects. Hence the artist's transference attaches to a huge variety of *topoi* handed on that may be arranged and rearranged, varied and deformed and revised in just the ways we see in the Messerschmidt pieces. There is continuity, yet with deep differences, between the official court art, with all its aesthetic details, and the studio busts, with all their aesthetic details. To understand the studio busts in the sense of allowing our countertransference to become part of a full response, we require both art-historical and psychoanalytic interpretations. For they are derived from forces operative in the artist's work as artist, and they are operative in the countertransference which is our response to the artist's transference.

To be sure, as Norman Holland suggests, every interpreter has private needs, some of them ideological in nature, that can be satisfied by a particular use of the psychoanalytic interpretation, for the psychoanalytic comes forward with observations that can be fitted into different kinds of explanatory systems.

Such a variety of uses to which psychoanalytic interpretations can be put is itself a part of the grand history of the philosophy of art, whose manifold interpretations of objects it is the art historian's task to chronicle. In that regard, Kris' interpretation of the Messerschmidt busts is in all likelihood influenced by the modern preoccupation with the medium in its own expressiveness, as expressed in the Boccioni manifesto. That manifesto surely did not have a psychoanalytic interpretation in its formulation, yet it worked, perhaps unconsciously, in the art history that Kris produced. Because Kris failed to distinguish the iconography of the medium as a conscious goal of his interpretation, he slid back into a psychoanalysis of the artist, producing finally a study that is continuous with the sort Freud would have written had he interpreted the Messerschmidt busts. Yet Kris wanted to break out of that, and by taking his failed effort alongside the Wittkowers' criticism, we may be able to move away from the psychoanalysis of the artist to the psychoanalytic interpretation of the work of art. That, it seems to me, is the goal of a psychoanalytic theory of art.

To be sure, the observations of the art historians are necessary guides, for art history can state the shared artistic intent of a period and a place. But as we have seen, the shared artistic structures can be mobilized in the service of many systems of belief, thought, and fantasy. Which ones are at work in any one case calls upon the training of both art historians and psychoanalytically sensitive interpreters; and an interesting issue therefore emerges in the dispute between Kris and the Wittkowers: is there a reason to prefer psychoanalytic training to other sorts that might be given the art historian? I shall come back to this question in chapter 5, but for the moment let me say simply that whatever theoretical stance is taken by art history, the psychoanalytic account of a work makes demands upon interpretation that are different from the demands of other theories. A psychoanalytic account by an art historian requires a high degree of self-consciousness, as well as deep knowledge about period and tradition. All theory calls for training and preparation for application to cases; the question then is whether the training that psychoanalytic theory calls for is worth the effort. The answer here is that it can open up to historical inquiry aspects of enactments which otherwise would be uninterpreted.

This challenge confronts the clinical as well as the art historical use of psychoanalytic theory. The challenge confronting the clinician—and it applies as well to those who would come to interpret works of art—was described by Freud in the following way when he reflected upon the preparation of patients to use their own dreams constructively:

What is in question, evidently, is the establishment of a psychical state which, in its distribution of psychical energy (that is, of mobile attention), bears some analogy to the state before falling asleep. . . . As we fall asleep, "involuntary ideas" emerge, owing to the relaxation of a certain deliberate (and no doubt also critical) activity which we allow to influence the course of our activity while we are awake. . . . As the involuntary ideas emerge they change into visual and acoustic images . . . the patient follow[s] the involuntary thoughts which now emerge . . . [and] retain the character of ideas. *In this way the "involuntary" ideas are transformed into "voluntary" ones.*[7]

The processes of interpreting dreams and works of art share certain characteristics; in both, a variety of visual and acoustic images emerge into consciousness. These objects often function as ideas, but ideas over which the receiver of the ideas has at first no control. Control is gained in the clinical situation under the guidance of the clinician; in the encounter with art, control is gained through wide experience, knowledge, and the capacity to respond to the right things in the right way. The phrase "the right things in the right way" is not meant to evade the issue of competence, but to stress the development in the observer of sensitivity to a wide range of demands that are expressed in feelings of fittingness and requiredness. By introducing the terms "fittingness" and "requiredness" I am borrowing from the perceptual analyses of Gestalt psychology descriptions of felt needs in the presence of objects like works of art. In part the feelings of what is fitting and not fitting, what is required and what is not required, are learned from the study of art history, but art history tends to "rationalize" the visual and acoustic images, treating them as remote from the psychic life in which they originate. The psychic life, however, is there in the work which in its structure exercises a control over the thought and the correct response. The formal structures of art both constrict and free the artist; the art historian tends to emphasize the constrictions, while the psychoanalytic interpreter emphasizes the freedom of creativity. Both, however, fail to apprehend the object in its full functioning as a cultural event participating in a tradition. I shall return to this aspect of art in the last chapter.

To be sure, the purposes and goals of clinical self-scrutiny are different from the purposes of art; yet art itself stands as a paradigm for inward search and outward expression. Art makes an object in the public world. I think that Freud's case histories had, for him, a similar aim, and that may account for the ways in which he wrote about art. The therapist, if sufficiently gifted, can make the process of the involuntary-become-voluntary into a formal organization that might have a public life outside the consulting room. Freud agrees with many idealistic philosophers in making aesthetic experience and the work of art a paradigm for consummatory experiences. It is not in the patient's performance that we are to find the artistic, but it might be found in the case history which, as I have already said, comes into its own as a genre in the late nineteenth century. From the case history valuable things have been learned which do apply to the close study of art.

In both the analysis of dreams and art the interpreter must learn to pay close attention to the minutest details of consciousness and all that can be recollected. The sensitivity to detail has application to our understanding of art, for the psychoanalytic method makes clear that the seemingly insignificant, least-emphasized elements of art are important points around which meaningful events may cluster.

In his essay on the *Moses* of Michelangelo, Freud compares his method of dream interpretation to that of the art historian Morelli, who directed us to observe the least details of painting. Pretending to be an art historian himself, Freud used the essay to draw parallels between psychoanalysis and art history:

Long before I had any opportunity of hearing about psychoanalysis, I learned that a Russian art-connoisseur, Ivan Lermolieff, had caused a revolution in the art galleries of Europe by questioning the authorship of many pictures, showing how to distinguish copies from originals with certainty, and constructing hypothetical artists for those works whose former supposed authorship had been discredited. He achieved this by insisting that attention should be diverted from the general impression and main features of a picture, and by laying stress on the significance of minor details, of things like the drawing of the fingernails, of the lobe of an ear, of halos and such unconsidered trifles which the copyist neglects to imitate and yet which every artist executes in his own characteristic way. I was then greatly interested to learn that the Russian pseudonym concealed the identity of an Italian physician called Morelli, who died in 1891. . . . It seems to me that his method of inquiry is closely related to the technique of psychoanalysis. It, too, is accustomed to divine secret and concealed things from the despised or unnoticed features, from the rubbish-heap, as it were, of our observations.[8]

Just as the art historian shares with the psychoanalyst the acuity to render details meaningful, so art history as a discipline extends its range to include that which falls into the class of unnoticed and neglected elements of art. Psychoanalytic sensitivity has contributed greatly to our ability to understand heretofore ignored or neglected elements in language and in visual symbolism. But it must be kept in mind that psychoanalytic inquiry can begin at the level of the obvious—large plot and scene—as well as at the stylistically minuscule. The task of interpretation most challenging is to relate the two aspects to one another.[9]

The foregoing descriptions of psychoanalytic method at work suggest that the process of interpretation presupposes a two-step response to art:

1. The first step calls upon us to develop a disposition to let works of art pass in and out of consciousness, with the purpose of learning to replace the involuntary with insight and control. Freud instructs us to enlarge our sensitivity, to become willing to entertain feelings and thoughts that traditionally have been considered inappropriate to the response elicited by works of art. In soliciting our openness, psychoanalytic theory attempts to create parallel circumstances in both artist and audience. Just as the artist creates out of openness to his conscious and unconscious thoughts, so the audience must learn to be responsive with a like availability of psychic content.

2. The second step establishes an interpretation of the work of art. Once the fullness of psychic response has been achieved, a centering, focusing, separating out of elements must occur. An analysis of symbolic content, both representational and non-representational, takes place. The perceiver asks what a particular event, theme, element, form "means." To understand the aim of this step, we must consider the concept *expression*, which in psychoanalytic usage involves the move from manifest to latent content.

II Psychoanalytic interpretations often begin with the question What does x express? This locution is common in expression theories of art; it presupposes that the work of art presents itself in a language, some parts of which are symbols whose meanings remain hidden, even though there is an available manifest sense. Expression is established when the manifest sense provides the initial given from which the observer can go to a remote latent content. The latent, upon interpretation, will be found to be a kind of thought. Recall the statement in "The History of the Psychoanalytic Movement": "Dreams are

merely *a form of thinking.*" This generalization was applied to
the latent content of art, folktales, fairy stories, myths, and many
other kinds of cultural objects.

A good example of the psychoanalytic use of expression can
be found in Freud's essay "The Theme of the Three Caskets,"
which attempts to interpret a theme that appears in several
different kinds of stories.[10] Although the literary forms are
diverse (fairy story, myth, and drama), the basic theme is always the same—i.e., a man must make a choice between one
of three women. Sometimes, as in the myth of Paris, it is explicitly three women; sometimes, as in Shakespeare's *The Mer-
chant of Venice*, the three women are symbolically represented
by caskets; and sometimes, as in *King Lear,* they are daughters. Freud enjoyed, somewhat in the manner of Lévi-Strauss,
tracing the various forms and manifestations of symbolic
themes. In "The Theme of the Three Caskets" he asks, "What
is expressed by the three women, and by the choice?" Freud
answers that the choice of one of three women expresses a
number of thoughts. (1) It expresses a common life situation
in which a man must deal with three women in his life, the
three to be interpreted as mother, wife, and death. (2) It also
expresses the anxiety we all feel toward death, and attempts to
cope with that anxiety by transforming (through negation)
death into that which is most beautiful and therefore freely
chosen. (3) It transforms the fearful, ugly death into the beautiful, desirable woman. (4) The story also expresses a fateful-
ness we all recognize in the passage through life toward death.
(5) The version of the theme in *King Lear,* in its similarity to
the other versions, allows us to interpret the character of Cordelia: "Cordelia is death," Freud asserts in an identity that is
startling.[11]

With that identification, through the use of the copula *is,*
Freud sums up a great deal of the kinds of interpretations psychoanalytic theory makes when it is applied to art. Cordelia is
perceived manifestly as a character with a set of qualities we

can readily discover through observing her behavior. But to add to those the noun *death* appears far-fetched indeed. What Freud assumes in making this identification is that the manifest content relates to a latent content, and that we are able to go from manifest to latent through a consideration of the total symbolic situation which is the drama *King Lear* in an expanded sense that we usually refer to as an "interpretation" of *King Lear*. The method of interpretation is in part a translation—i.e., we translate the figure Cordelia into the idea of death; partly an expansion—i.e., we add the idea of death to the other ideas we entertain about Cordelia; and partly a transformation—i.e., we now see the Lear–Cordelia relationship differently, from a new perspective, as it were.

To assert "Cordelia is death" joins the manifest element of the drama *King Lear* with a latent theme of the play whose manifest presentations are so numerous that we see them woven into every thought and assertion of the play. To say "Cordelia is death" not only constitutes an interpretation of the final scene of the play, but also asserts that the play is *truly* or *really* about death, and consistent in its preoccupation with the reality of death. This should alert us to the fact that psychoanalytic theory of art, in making the manifest–latent distinction, is introducing a distinction of a philosophical kind between appearance and reality. In psychoanalytic theory "reality" does not refer exclusively to the external world of "physical reality"; but rather it refers to the internal reality which Freud refers to as "psychological reality." From this point of view, manifest and latent constitutes a contrast between that given to perception in experience, and that revealed as the psychological reality through an interpretation on psychoanalytic principles.[12]

Freud's discussion of *King Lear* is of course but a brief example in an essay devoted to a larger theme, but his observations here, as in other places, completely overlook the political themes so central to the work. This neglect gives me another opportunity to relate the psychosexual and the political as we ought to do if we are to develop a psychoanalytic philosophy of art.

In the play *King Lear* there is a close connection between Lear's psychological preoccupations and his efforts to be a good ruler. The opening scene of the drama displays the conflict, and in itself indicates a way to bring together Freud's cultural and aesthetic insights.

Lear has two purposes in his division of the kingdom, of one of which he is aware, and to which he has given much thought; the other of which he is unaware, and which has a profound influence on his actions. The first we can properly call conscious, the second unconscious, purpose. Consciously Lear attempts to fulfill his obligations as a ruler: to preserve peace in the kingdom, establish continuity of rule, and publish his purpose that all may know his plan for political organization after his death. At the same time he struggles with a real political problem that comes a bit closer to the unconscious purposes. That is the problem of inheritance when the next generation is all daughters. Since a first-born son would inherit were there sons, the problem Lear has to cope with is complicated by there being only daughters. As Freud points out, this has a mythic content and has been dealt with many times in myth; but Freud fails to see the practical problem in political terms. Both the psychological and the political here require resolution.

Finally, Lear's actions show us that he is moved by unconscious needs that are personal and in conflict with the political obligations of a ruler. He has three daughters; only one does he love, and only one can be trusted. She is the youngest and about to be married, provided a husband can be persuaded to accept her. It is Lear's intention that a particular suitor be chosen (Burgundy) and that another (France) be rejected. This has political implications that are far-reaching, for Burgundy is the most powerful continental ruler, and a liaison between Lear's daughter Cordelia and Burgundy would ally England's ruler with the most powerful ruler abroad. Such an alliance would also insure that the other daughters (Regan and Goneril) would never be able to overwhelm Cordelia, and thus the safety of the kingdom would be assured.[13]

Yet in the creation of this alliance Lear does strange things. It has often been said that Lear demonstrates either bad judgment or senility by his demand that his three daughters declare their love for him. In psychoanalytic terms such a demand is "over-determined"; that is to say, Lear has many motives for his demand, and seeks several outcomes to the performances he wishes the courtiers to witness. Politically, a declaration of love in a public setting before all the ranks in rule would be understood as an expression of fealty. In declarations of love, the daughters express their acceptance of the division of the kingdom, and their dedication to their father's continued presence in the kingdom. For remember that Lear plans to live with Cordelia with one hundred knights, a formidable fighting force.

To live with Cordelia, to be king yet not king, to see his kingdom as it will be and as it is after his death, projects, as in a fantasy, an odd and really an impossible state of affairs. It is not only impossible to survive one's own death; it is politically most unusual to give away your kingdom before you are dead. This contradiction well expresses the contradictory state of mind and affect from which Lear suffers. It is a clue to the deeper conflicts that trouble him and in the end prevent him from being a successful ruler.

Thus when Lear demands that his daughters declare their love for him he is doing several things at once. Consciously he seeks a public expression of fealty, an acceptance of his power and his plan. Goneril and Regan and their husbands are supposed to accept thankfully a third of the kingdom. Yet he asks them to accept thirds that are in two ways less than the third for Cordelia. First, they are geographically separated, Cornwall's domain being in the south, Albany's being in the north;

Cordelia's "third" is actually larger and is in the middle separating the less dependable sisters from one another. Second, not only is Cordelia's third greater, her marriage as planned by Lear will ally her to the greatest continental power. In all this then Lear is hardly treating the three daughters equally. Yet he has a real political problem to solve, and given the natures of the three his plan is canny and well thought out.

However, since the delcaration of love has other motives and purposes, we can expect a conflict to develop, for the "darker purpose" is not what Lear thinks it is. The conflict comes about with Cordelia's refusal to declare her love as Lear wishes it; she understands that the request hides a purpose that would destroy her. From that perception and its dreadful rebuke to Lear the tragedy flows. He first would deny her marriage to Burgundy—or to any man—since he wants Cordelia for himself. He is again frustrated by France's willingness to have Cordelia, who accepts him. That this betrayal is an ultimate rejection to Lear becomes clear in his immediate political response, for he does the one thing his plan was calculated to avoid, thus contradicting both his obvious outer and his most hidden inner intentions; he divides the kingdom in two. By giving Goneril and Regan equal portions and setting them in a position he will supposedly control by living alternately with each accompanied by his one hundred knights, he makes inevitable a conflict between the two powers. Given Goneril's and Regan's temperaments, they cannot brook one another's presence. And therefore Lear's plan to preserve the peace is transformed into a plan to guarantee war.

Such a reversal, in miniature the very tragic reversal itself, shows how much deeper and psychologically how much more complex Lear's purposes were than we at first suspected. The play does its work with remarkable economy; within one scene of one act the whole political and affective orientation is reversed, the relationships of all the rulers and family turned upside down in the sense that manifest considerations become overwhelmed in latent considerations, and rational considerations drowned in instinctual demands.

The analysis of *King Lear* just presented illustrates the need, pointed out in chapter 2, for an integration of Freud's clincial and cultural writing. Provided as we are with an interpretation of Lear's quest and his complex relationship to public obligation and private need, to rule and to love, we lack the political which seems submerged in the psychosexual. There are political concerns expressed by the character King Lear which we shall find discussed in *Civilization and Its Discontents*. Here then is a case of interpretation calling for an integration of two consistently elaborated themes in Freud's thought. The tragedy itself poses the question of Freud's essay. Part III of *Civilization and Its Discontents* in fact summarizes and states the themes of *King Lear*: "the superior power of nature, the feebleness of our own bodies and the inadequacy of the regulations which adjust the mutual relationships of human beings in the family, the state and society. . . . As regards the third source, the social source of suffering, our attitude is a different one. We do not admit it at all: we cannot see why the regulations made by ourselves should not . . . be a protection and a benefit for every one of us. And yet, when we consider how unsuccessful we have been in precisely the field of prevention of suffering, a suspicion dawns upon us that here, too, a piece of unconquerable nature may lie behind—this time a piece of our own psychical constitution."[14]

This suspicion becomes a certainty as we watch *King Lear*, but an understanding of that revelation requires political as well as psychological insight. *Civilization and Its Discontents* goes on to deal with the political conflicts: "So . . . the two urges, the one towards personal happiness and the other towards union with other human beings, must struggle with each other in every individual; and so, also, the two processes of individual and of cultural development must stand in hostile opposition to each other and mutually dispute the ground."[15]

The full extent and various manifestations of this dispute are not developed in Freud's own writing. One manifestation, as I have argued, is in the art we call "tragedy," and it may be that every tragic drama has at its heart the "hostile opposition" of which Freud speaks. Whether that is so or not, the contribution of *Civilization and Its Discontents* is broader and more interesting than that. Human beings have a basic need to represent, to externalize, to set before themselves in forms of art the divisions, conflicts, and contradictions they find in themselves, in their actual needs and in their wish-fulfilling efforts to cope with their needs. In that respect works of art do not result simply from the sorts of frustrations Freud described in his early essay on the artist and daydreaming. Freud's own thought penetrated to a deeper level of human need and means to satisfy that need. In its greatest achievements, art enables human beings to examine and work through the conflicts between individuals and society, between the self and the political reality each one of us inhabits. Looking at psychoanalytic theory in this broader context allows us to overcome its own tendency to trivializing reductionism. Art is not simply a working through of the artists' problems and conflicts; it is a representation of universal communal conflicts in which everyone is entangled.

III *Civilization and Its Discontents,* I have argued, really does contribute to a general theory of the arts through its contribution to a theory of tragedy, and the study of tragedy helps to illuminate the conflicts *Civilization and Its Discontents* defines, and ultimately despairs of resolving. However, it seems to me that the arts themselves, when conceived of as a class of enactments, do contribute to a possible resolution of the problems psychoanalytic theory struggled to subdue. We can readily see that the conflicts represented in tragic drama are often the sort Freud described in *Civilization and Its Dis-*

contents. All the plays we consider tragedies present a protagonist who seeks to make congruent and consistent inner wishes, needs, gratifications, desires with the public obligations to others—to society at large—that he sustains as a forceful presence in the community.

Put in this broader context, psychoanalytic theory must ask, What is the effect on an audience of seeing these conflicts that tragedy represents? Since civilization, Freud argued, rests upon repression, and the norms of conduct that presuppose repression, the "message" of tragedy could very well be destructive to social coherence. The very impossibility of accommodating private and public—one of the deep truths discovered by tragedy—could lead some members of the audience to severe depression, wanhope and, ultimately, indifference to political values. Plato saw this, and argued that tragedy ought not be allowed; Aristotle saw it too, and argued that the knowledge delivered by tragedy could be liberating and civilizing rather than anarchic. The bringing together of this classical debate with Freud's reflections in *Civilization and Its Discontents* can lead to a much more satisfactory theory of tragedy than those we have so far formulated.

While *Civilization and Its Discontents* asks if the price we pay for civilization may be too high, the nature of tragic drama as set forth in both classical and psychoanalytic sources suggests that art itself—and perhaps especially tragic drama—may be of use in resolving or at least coming to an understanding of the conflict between individuals and their cultural obligations. May it not be the case that art ameliorates the conflict that it itself depicts? A society that encourages the arts, especially the more serious arts such as tragedy, deals with the deepest psychic conflicts, and in so doing helps the individual cope with the conflicts of growing up as a member both of a family and of society.

This view, which I attribute to an imaginative reconstruction of *Civilization and Its Discontents*, was explored by Aristotle in the *Poetics,* where he declares that "one must not seek any and every kind of pleasure from tragedy, but only the one proper to it" (53b11). To defend the view that there is a *pleasure* in witnessing dire, frightening, sometimes horrifying events places the *Poetics* in a tradition that psychoanalytic theory could easily accommodate. The position Aristotle was attacking was, of course, that maintained by Plato, and later by Augustine and Rousseau, that the representation of painful events, and the feelings of pleasure connected to witnessing them, was a sign of human depravity. If it could be demonstrated that there is a right kind of response to tragedy, then the attack mounted by a politically puritanical vision of communal life might be mitigated, and a way made for a kind of representational action that has positive political consequence.

That tragedy concerns itself with the political was recognized both by Plato and Aristotle, with different conclusions drawn as to the justifiability of a political content that saw deeply into the grave difficulty in achieving just rule. Plato thought it necessary to hide the pessimistic content of tragic action from the community; Aristotle argued that such content delivered a deep and politically strengthening vision. Tragedy, so it was understood in the tradition of classical philosophy, turns upon a deep, pervasive, ineradicable conflict, that between private need and public obligation. The first is sexual, the second moral and political. Its most obvious example is the history of Oedipus, but we see the same conflict in all the tragic heros—e.g., Lear, Hamlet, Othello—in different forms, with different developmental histories. But in all tragedy, and in much serious drama, the conflict is clear: private sexual need and public political obligation inevitably come into conflict. Simply stated, the tragic plots gain inextinguishable energy and force from a conflict that is unresolvable, because each side of the need cannot be satisfied without violation of the other.

King Lear cannot both divide the kingdom and possess Cordelia. Oedipus cannot both rule as king and possess his mother as his wife. No resolution of these conflicts is possible; tragic suffering, as Aristotle pointed out, follows from these conflicts with inevitability. We might call the well-made plot a syllogism of suffering. Grasping such a structure of events in itself gives pleasure, the pleasure of recognition, but more than that, the inevitable and unresolvable conflict arouses a deeper pleasure in us, for we respond to it with recognition of a pervasive human prohibition, and with our own sense of god-like power. We survey the tragic plot as if it were ours to dominate and control; we achieve immortal prescience, and that permits us to celebrate suffering as evidence of our now transcendent (although woefully transitory) powers. We seek to resolve an inevitable conflict of our own nature with a fantasy of suprahuman omnipotence.

There remains, however, an unanswered question regarding our capacity to find pleasure in representations of the painful. Why is it that we respond with a truly aesthetic delight to something which in real life would be both morally and politically unacceptable? Psychoanalytic theory not only helps to define the nature of the tragic conflict; it also suggests ways in which the conflict is ameliorated and internalized, for the relationship of audience to drama is one that participates in the larger complex relationship of transference, already described. Participation in a dramatic presentation—one of a class of events I have analyzed in the previous chapter as "enactments"—confronts the audience with events and feelings that have locations in the experience, conscious and unconscious, of each observer. The plot, characters, thought, scenes of suffering in the play reproduce and represent in metaphoric form varieties of affects, beliefs, wishes, fears, anxieties, hopes, and fantasy entertainments whose interconnections establish a psychosexual history for each person. The dramatic presence, however, achieves more than a mere mirroring; it "works through" the events to a resolution and coerces the audience to accord acceptance to the manifestly unacceptable. In that resolution a "katharsis," not simply of feeling but of belief and of thought about persons and events, becomes established in the private and public obligations whose competing claims must be recognized. The conclusion of a well-made plot then allows the recognitions to occur as part of a process that has affinities to the process of therapy. Indeed, it was one of Aristotle's deepest insights to see that tragic drama is in some ways like, but in a most fundamental way unlike, the ecstatic postures and wish-fulfillments of the bacchantic celebrants. The difference lies in this: for the bacchantic celebrants the ecstatic state must be sought again and again, while the well-made tragic plot effected a more permanent recognition in a changed attitude toward the self and the state and the impossibility of satisfactorily adjudicating their competing claims.[16]

In other contexts Freud would refer to that outcome as a form of sublimation (*Sublimierung*), the condition in which an instinct, sexual in nature, is realized in a goal that is nonsexual, at least manifestly. Thus, the tragic drama receives great energy from sexual sources, and realizes a redirection of their aim and goal in analyzing them in a thoroughly political set of events. But to make this comparison between an insight of a classical text and psychoanalytic theory is simply to reiterate an observation of Freud's, that psychoanalysis was by no means the first thinking to recognize the deeper interrelationships of the sexual and the political. Both Aristotle and Freud would agree that a high achievement of culture was to realize the sublimating power of serious artistic representations.

Psychoanalytic explanations can be joined to the classical speculations to account for the mysterious evocation tragedy brings about through which an audience enjoys painful affects. The force first manifests itself in the maturational project of the human being who as child moves from "the third area" to full cultural functioning. Here I once again draw upon the thought of D. W. Winnicott, as well as more traditional theory, to account for the developmental possibility of tragedy.[17]

My elaboration of Winnicott's views suggests that an enactment, such as tragic drama, is one of the ways an individual has to move out from the immediacy of internal and family conflict to the realities that the familiar plots present. If we consider tragic plots in terms of their familiarity, their repetitions, their continuity with some of the first stories a child hears, the early transitional objects stand in a sequence in which the objects we think of as *art* relate developmentally to the childhood manipulation of objects in play with the parents. There, frightening accounts produce real terror which can be modified as the representational nature of narration becomes understood. As the transitional object becomes work of art, shared by the community as a whole, it retains in some respects the properties of the earlier objects, and relies upon psychological conditions laid down in early years, conditions that function in later years when the transitional object has been succeeded by things like tragic plots.

The earlier condition, however, remains in some respects present and operative, for tragic plots are surrounded by much the same risks as early transitional tales: the hearer feels anxiety and suffers the painful affects that Aristotle referred to as "pity" and "fear." Yet the overall experience possesses deep and abiding satisfactions that make taking the risks worthwhile.

In two late papers Freud speculated on the psychological process by which the ambivalences of our experience with tragedy may be understood, and our willingness to take the risk of tragedy accounted for. Introducing the terms "split" and "splitting," Freud suggested in the uncompleted "An Outline of Psychoanalysis," and in the fragment "Splitting of the Ego in the Process of Defense," that we possess and use "splitting" as a means to cope with fearful and threatening situations.[18] "Two psychical attitudes," he writes, "have been formed instead of a single one—one, the normal one, which takes account of reality, and another which under the influences of the instincts detaches the ego from reality. The two exist alongside of each other." Splitting of the ego, Freud goes on to say, characterizes many psychological processes, and we often find, especially in psychosis and neurosis, that "two different attitudes, contrary to each other and independent of each other," are to be found in many interactions between the ego and external reality.[19]

Developing these views in a posthumously published fragment, Freud points out that in children we see the capacity to tolerate "a conflict between the demand by the instinct and the prohibition by reality," by taking two positions simultaneously and therefore splitting the ego. The child both turns away from reality, and turns toward reality, thus resolving what appears to be a contradiction with simultaneous affirmations: experience countenances and finds room for both A and not A, or for the contraries A and B, through maintaining a fantasy construal alongside a realistic construal of the world.[20]

Transitional objects, in the limited sense explored by Winnicott, and in the broader sense introduced in this essay, become the first cultural objects through splitting. The participants assume two positions simultaneously: they recognize the terror and the suffering of the action, as they also deny the reality of the presentation because it is a representation. Storytelling, whether in the simple mode of familial play or in the sophisticated mode of serious drama, relies upon the process of splitting for the special pleasure it engenders.

One way in which that pleasure is encouraged and allowed to manifest itself is through the very content and structure of the dramatic plots themselves, for they too employ the process of splitting. In tragic drama splitting of objects and of selves occurs in many fascinating ways; the conflict between private sexual need and public political obligation splits persons and actions into seemingly irreconcilable dualities that yet must find a possible coexistence in the plot, and in so doing call upon the audience to participate in the splitting and the reconciliation. As we witness the plot, we are ourselves brought into the var-

ious bifurcations which enable us to maintain a dual set of responses, holding at once the painful and the pleasurable in an
unresolved tension which is also a coordination. The affective
life of the audience now must arrange these dualities into an
acceptable response. Just how is that brought about?

Acceptable response refers to the pleasure peculiar to scenes
of suffering that conclude tragic narratives. This is a pleasure
unlike the pleasure of revenge, unlike the pleasure of simple
excitement, unlike the pleasure we take in the beautiful. For
in all these respects, in terms of these values—values of seeing
an enemy fall, of entertainment, of the aesthetic—the pleasure
Aristotle referred to is distinct, it is the pleasure appropriate to
tragedy: we seek not any and every kind of pleasure from tragedy, but only the one it demands.

Since tragic drama both elicits and directs powerful feelings
that are in other contexts painful, to experience the pleasure
appropriate to tragedy suggests that the feelings are manipu-
lated in a special way peculiar to this kind of representation;
and it is not satisfactory to say that the pleasure we experience
derives from the representational as such, for there are many
representational effects that are revolting and thoroughly unacceptable. There must be a way that the tragic representations work for us and in us that will help to explain the pleasure we take in scenes of suffering. I propose that the process
of splitting, as sketched out in the above discussion, accounts
for the pleasure appropriate to tragedy.

To be sure, we discover the pleasure appropriate to tragedy
at a late stage in our cultural maturation; it succeeds a much
more simplified and simplifying view of ourselves that begins
to take shape in our commerce with transitional objects. Each
of the events embodied in tragic plots occurs over and over
again in the stories we hear as we grow up.

The central cultural conflict that energizes tragic plots, the
irresolvability of private sexual need and public political obligation, drives the action forward to a disclosure of the full in-

congruity humans must forever struggle to resolve. In that life-long, and indeed historically constant, effort, an internal bifurcation expresses itself in the splitting of persons and ob-jects. In taking up splitting as a part of its own representational concerns, tragedy separates out the painful and the pleasurable in plots so that we witnesses are led to perform the same ka-thartic clarification in ourselves.

Through the psychoanalytic concept of splitting, the classi-cal concept of *Katharsis* assumes a broader application as we endeavor to establish the implications of that seemingly simple phrase, "the pleasure appropriate to tragedy," that Aristotle for-mulated as partial answer to Plato. The developmental trajec-tory of our quest to achieve wholeness in ourselves as part of our participation in both historical tradition and present politi-cal life finds support in many different kinds of cultural under-takings.

It should follow from the psychoanalytic contribution to an understanding of tragedy, that Freud's writings on culture co-vertly imply the importance to civilization of enlarging the in-fluence and availability of serious art forms. It seems to me that the psychoanalytic reflections on art and culture imply a possible therapeutic force in some of the arts; but Freud did not explicitly consider the place of art in society in these terms.

To establish the relationship of art to the developmental se-quence of growing up, we must avoid simple reductionism. Ul-timately, what makes artists and their work important psy-choanalytically is their contribution to and critique of culture. Therefore, in Freud's own terms, though he did not say this, it may be the case that the arts are the most important social instruments for achieving both individual and cultural matu-ration. Insisting as I have upon the necessity to integrate the psychosexual and the cultural in Freud's thought in order to allow psychoanalytic theory to realize all it is capable of as a philosophy of art, I must here refer once again to the earlier discussion of chapter 3. As I argued in chapter 3, the analysis of cultural objects which followed upon Freud's speculations established the deep importance for cultural functioning of cultural objects such as the ones I have been discussing here. The importance of those objects to an understanding of the psychoanalytic theory of art and culture is to be found in their very substance, for the greatest of them represent the interrelationship of objects and culture. Thus the quest undertaken by the character Lear when *King Lear* opens is precisely the quest we, as witnesses, have been undertaking in our lives—whether consciously recognized or not—and a quest we enact within ourselves as we witness the enactment. The failure of Lear's quest does not imply the failure of our own in the developmental process, though indeed the drama may make a statement we accept as true about the possibility of success in the quest we all enter upon in our political and psychosexual lives. As witnesses to the enactment, we respond to and use the enactment in ways that are foreclosed to the characters enacting. That very difference between characters within the representation and witnesses outside it is one of the powers of the enactment to bring about a transitional move, conveying us from our self-enclosed consciousness to remote areas both within ourselves (the unconscious) and without ourselves (the reality of nature and the communal life). Transitional experience depends upon more than the single object and the single experience of a single performance. Witnesses differ from characters in this respect: witnesses possess not simply the one enactment, but many enactments within the tradition, and many instances of the particular drama *King Lear*. The characters within possess knowledge of some other objects in the tradition, and if they do, they express that knowledge in the words they utter and the situations they find themselves in. They may refer to, quote, represent, imitate other enactments. What the characters know enters into our response as witnesses; yet what we know as witnesses always surpasses the wide spectrum of affects and the details of knowledge delivered in the single case because we have access to other cases.

The single case yet performs the transitional function: it delivers us to the Lear-world and its allied objects; it returns us from the Lear-world with whatever fragment of that presence we have been able to break off. In time, with successive reflections and comparisons, the tradition we possess is reshaped by the succession of objects and insights we have been able to inform with the Lear-presence. Placing that successfully is the task of interpretation, and that task is accomplished through the help of various—perhaps many—theories. No one theory can be designated as the one to meet all the needs of the object and our experience as witnesses. Tradition lays an obligation upon us to master the theories the objects demand, the theories through which our tradition realizes itself. Among those, the psychoanalytic has its own guidance to give, its interpretations to make, its truths to serve. That interpretations serve truth is itself a belief of the tradition we possess.

IV In the idealistic tradition of philosophy of art, theories of expression are intimately related to theories of truth. The claim is made that the expressed content of art can be understood, in part, as a set of true propositions. This is sometimes put in a shorthand way as "art reveals truth." Thus, in the example of *King Lear* just presented, the psychoanalytic interpretation of the play maintains the latent content to be not merely the "play-thoughts," analogous to the "dream-thoughts," but also to be true. The method enables the interpreter to translate the thought and the action into propositional forms whose truth or falsity is then to be assayed. Idealistic theories treat cultural products, such as drama, as avenues to both outer physical and inner psychological reality.

The term "reality," like the term "truth," is difficult to apply to art, yet just as expression theories of art refer to claims to truth on the part of art objects, so they treat art objects as expressing the way things really are. If art reveals truth, then it must describe or represent some aspect of reality, things as they *really* are. In Hegel's theory, cultural products express the deeper, underlying forces that move historical events, as well as the deeper levels of consciousness, unavailable to the peoples who made the objects. Freud would agree with Hegel that the right method of interpretation could lay bare the underlying psychological reality which expressions of all kinds might hide. The problem that psychoanalytic theory faces, and one to which Freud devoted much thought, is how to recognize the references to reality in the manifest material of works of art, and then to determine how the expressed material could be interpreted, for interpretations should lead back to the reality that the expression obliquely represents.

In considering the various ways this relationship of expression to underlying reality might occur, Freud distinguishes two basic references to reality that his clinical practice revealed. He described these two kinds of reference as "loss of reality" and "substitute for reality."[21] A theory of expression seizes upon the junctures in psychic life where reality is either lost or distorted or symbolically represented in metaphorical and analogical forms. Thus Freud wrote in "The Loss of Reality in Neurosis and Psychosis,"

Whereas the new, imaginary external world of a psychosis attempts to put itself in the place of external reality, that of a neurosis, on the contrary, is apt, like the play of children, to attach itself to a piece of reality—a different piece from the one against which it has to defend itself—and to lend that piece a special importance and a secret meaning which we (not always quite appropriately) call a *symbolic* one. Thus we see that in both neurosis and psychosis there comes into consideration the question not only of a *loss of reality* but also of a *substitute for reality*.[22]

The task of analysis is to recover the lost reality, and the way to do this is to understand the symbolic representations in terms of which reality and its substitutes are used in the psychic economy of the individual. In an analogous way, psychoanalytic theory confronts cultural objects and treats them as symbolic representations of both physical and psychological reality, realities that have been lost or displaced through substitution. The psychoanalytic view of enactments as systems of expression always regards the object in terms of the metaphoric and symbolic structures that call for interpretation. In the process of interpretation the represented substitutes for reality should emerge, and the realities they hide should be found. But now the method of restoration through interpretation confronts greater complexities, for where works of art are concerned the loss of reality and the substitute for reality are losses and substitutions that occur *within the work of art.* Freud's method was to extend psychoanalytic theory from the clinical to the artistic without taking into account the special needs of the domain of enactments. When psychoanalysis turns to objects one of the questions that must be asked is the degree to which a particular object establishes its own reality without the need to compel referential inferences outside itself, and without the need to make an analogy with psychotic substitutions.

These are subtle differences between the consulting room and the response to enactments; the analyst must be able to make discriminations between reality and its various affirmations and negations *within* the object. Psychoanalytic studies of art frequently make the mistake of jumping outside the work to the life of the artist, yet when the purpose of the inquiry is to give a psychoanalytic interpretation *of art,* the object itself and its own establishment of reality must be the focus of attention. In this section I shall illustrate the way in which psychoanalytic inquiry, when not autobiographical in its intention, can search for representations of reality in the work in order to evaluate the claims to truth made on behalf of latent content. My example is a short story by Herman Melville.

"The Paradise of Bachelors and the Tartarus of Maids" presents two scenes, each in part realistic, in part fantastic. The problem is to achieve coherence both within and between the two sections of the story. I shall examine the various internal references, beginning with the narration in its literal description.

Literal references are clear: a bachelors' club in London, a paper mill in New England. The scenes are differentiated by the text's division into two parts. The only explicit reference from one part to another is the first person storyteller's statement that as he leaves the dark valley of the New England mill, he thinks of the warm, cozy rooms in the London bachelors' club. Why the two events are told as parts of one story is never stated; yet it is clear that each scene comes out of deeply private recollections.

Despite the realistic descriptions, the events recounted are almost blatantly multireferential. Perhaps the most obvious example—one, by the way, I have found many readers overlook—is the paper-making machine and the paper-making rooms described in a language that one, it would seem, must recognize as descriptions of gestation and birth. The references are so explicitly referential in two modes that rather than call the description "symbolic," the reader might think of the story as an allegory. Industrial and biological processes are described at the same time. This use of language is a narrative clue—hardly subtle—that directs the reader to seek complexities of representation and reference throughout the story.

The symbolic description in part two, once recognized, requires the reader to reexamine the descriptions throughout the story, and they, too, turn out to be symbolic substitutions and displacements of a psychosexual kind. There is a puzzling contrast between the blatantly sexual description of women—not only through the factory, but also through the landscape—and the almost totally asexual description of the men at the bachelors' party. In part one we are present at a familial, warm, cozy gathering in every respect the opposite of the icy mill. Yet in the midst of the cold of winter there is the heat of reproductive sexuality, and in the warmth of gluttonous camaraderie there is the chill of sexual abstinence.

Once the multiplicities and contrarieties of reference are established, the reader can be led by the narrative into the deeper and deeper unconscious of the text. The experience of reading this story is one of exploration, and it soon becomes apparent that the process Freud wrote about in the clinical setting appears here as well: loss of reality, and substitute for reality is the deepest metaphoric demand made upon the reader. We can respond to the narrative techniques by which loss and substitution are realized without going outside the text to the artist.

The two distinctly different scenes in the story are complementary fantasies, but exactly how they relate to one another is puzzling. One similarity seems fairly clear: they each share in infantile fantasies about sexual differences and about biological beliefs held in early life, and the latent presence of such beliefs in adult life. Yet as soon as that is said, the demands of the story assert themselves, for the narrative events themselves recover within their own telling a lost world that reconstitutes itself in recollections. That is, at every stage of analysis, in which the reader sees as it were the psychoanalytic interpretation exemplified, the story becomes the theory, so that we must be careful to let the story explain itself, and not impose a gratuitous explanation upon it.

The past of infantile fantasies, so vividly resurrected in the two separate scenes, is in one respect forever lost—as lost as are these bizarre happenings which the narrator claims to have befallen. Yet in another respect, the infantile fantasies are always present and operative, as indeed they are in the story which recovers the past that is buried and sets it up in the present. Thus the reader recognizes the events in their immediacy of presentation, and can respond to them with the accumulation of repressed fantasy and present revivification through the powers of the descriptions. And just as the recollections exist inside the story, and side-by-side in their odd juxtaposition, so in the recollections of the reader, however unconscious, there are complementary interpretations of sexuality which are embedded in a larger adult matrix. The two parts of the story are not simply successive, but co-exist and must be read each with the other in mind.

Although the two parts of the story obviously are "about" unmarried men and women ("bachelors" and "maids"), the closeness of marriage and babies is a hovering threat. The Paradise of Bachelors, the story tells, is to be found by turning off "Fleet Street—where the Benedick tradesmen are hurrying by, with ledger-lines ruled along their brows; thinking upon the rise of bread and the fall of babies." The lined brow appears again in the Tartarus of Maids: "I looked upon the first girl's brow, and saw it was ruled and wrinkled." Careworn, exhausted from serving the machine which is really a gestation mechanism, the women in part two of the story lack all the felicity, companionship, and childlike freedom of the bachelors, yet they are maids, so the suffering is not from actual childbearing but from a universal female condition.

Despite the repressions of sexuality, both the bachelors and the maids are enslaved by sexual drives. The bachelors have regressed to a condition of infantile gratification, and the maids are enslaved to a machine that is a baby-maker. Mature genital sexuality seems to be frightening and beyond the capacities of both bachelors and maids, though why that is so is not clear. In both vignettes, economic wealth and poverty, social class, old world and new world seem also to be decisive factors in determining the conditions of life, yet despite the coalescence of all these "causes," the more basic determining factor seems to be in the bachelors and the maids themselves. Therefore an interpretation of the story requires a careful separating out of conscious and unconscious thought as part of the narration itself. But in giving the interpretation we must not lose sight of the real world in which the characters live: it is at once psychosexual, social, economic.

The two parts of the narrative refer to each other as the repressed of each other. The setting of the Woedolor Mountain, where the seedsman goes to get paper packets for his seeds, is the New England landscape shaped as if it were the "invisible lowlands" of the female body, the fearful and repressed reality excluded from bachelor consciousness. The London club, representing physical sensuality totally removed from the women's work, hovers behind their enslavement, a vivid, preoccupied world whose gratifying physicality can never penetrate the factory fastness.

The seedsman penetrates the valley—described with anatomical precision as female genitals—to observe the baby-making machine trammel its servitors. Regarding that scene from the felicity of London, the males have realized a dream of grace in which the mother is present only as a solicitous and nurturing surrounding, and the "babies" are there fed. The men, having thoroughly repressed the reality of sexuality, have relegated it to the new world in its most ferocious season. It is within the story itself that the displacements, exclusions, substitutes, and interpreted events occur, as, for example, the New England winter has a reference to the denials of London.

Indeed, the winter of New England remains cold, distant, terrifying to the male warmth, sexual lability, and instinctive gratification that takes food for its object. The men have exiled baby-making to cold, distant valleys, overseen by impersonal seedsmen, while they cosset themselves in the oral love of feast and talk. That might be a "solution" to the anxieties of sexuality, indeed in the story it *is* a narrative solution, in the sense that it is a manifest fantasy to cover deeper narrative, latent, thoughts.

Each half is just that, half the story, half the "solution" to the problem, a half lacking its wholeness for which the reader must look to the other half, as men and women without each other are half the story of adult life. The untold half in each half is the repressed half which can be reconstituted through the presentations of the other half. The story halves itself in its telling, as in its title: the eschatological domains to which the men and women have been condemned by their denial of wholeness. If one were to inhabit the realms of the dead, one would be freed of living obligations; the story announces its commitment to fantasy by using "Paradise" and "Tartarus," yet there is a painful realism about the story that prevents the reader from relegating the two scenes to fantasy. Reality wears through the most artfully misleading manifest entertainment with which the story opens: a party given to pleasure. As we are entertained, the discomfort of human existence made whole, a reminder like a memento mori, keeps peering in.

The two halves of the story are reflections of each other as if reversals in a mirror of maturation. As recent psychoanalytic theory in its fascination with objects points out, the ways in which objects function for the individual are expressions of inner psychic organizations; and so too in this story, each half is an object for the other half, an object whose reversals are noted by the seedsman.

The mirror-like reversals of the two sections are manifest in settings, colors, seasons, characters, and, most important, language. Consider the two following passages, one from each section:

1. Not long after the cloth was drawn our host glanced significantly upon Socrates, who, solemnly stepping to a stand, returned with an immense convolved horn, a regular Jericho horn, mounted with polished silver, and otherwise chased and curiously enriched; not omitting two lifelike goatheads, with four more horns of solid silver, projecting from opposite sides of the mouth of the noble main horn.

2. Flaked all over with frozen sweat, white as a milky ram, his nostrils at each breath sending forth two horn-shaped shoots of heated respiration, Black, my good horse, but six years old, started at a sud-

den turn, where right across the track—not ten minutes fallen—an old distorted hemlock lay, darkly undulatory as an anaconda.

The horse mirrors the horn of snuff by being called "white as a milky ram" and by "sending forth two horn-shaped shoots" in the cold winter air. In both parts of the tale there is an animal presence that is alluded to but never explicitly allowed to come out. The guest at the bachelors' feast is slightly disturbed at the oxtail soup because it reminds him of "teamster's gads and the rawhides of ushers." References back and forth display the conscious and unconscious structuring and restructuring as dreams do through their repetitions. Each theme is sounded several times with different tonalities and articulations, now in a ceremonial propriety, now in an organic unseemliness. And yet with all those sexual references, there is no overt instinctual expression permitted.

In the Melville story there is some effort to make the language portray itself, to "speak" about itself as it narrates. The sentence structure exhibits important variation:

1. In mild meditation pace the cloisters; take your pleasure, sip your leisure, in the garden waterward; go linger in the ancient library; go worship in the sculptured chapel; but little have you seen, just nothing do you know, not the kernel have you tasted, till you dine among the banded Bachelors, and see their convivial eyes and glasses sparkle.

2. Conspicuously crowning a rocky bluff high to one side, at the cataract's verge, is the ruin of an old saw-mill, built in those primitive times when vast pines and hemlocks superabounded throughout the neighboring region. The black-mossed bulk of those immense, rough-hewn, and spike-knotted logs, here and there tumbled all together, in long abandonment and decay, or left in solitary, perilous projection over the cataract's gloomy brink, impart to this rude wooden ruin not only much of the aspect of one of rough-quarried stone, but also a sort of feudal, Rhineland and Thurmberg look, derived from the pinnacled wildness of the neighborhood scenery.

In the passage from section one the punctuation, choice of words, and the emphasis on physical activity animates the thought and the structure. Entertained, comforted, befriended as we will be at the bachelors' party, we anticipate all the joys in the language itself. But in just opposition to that use and structure, the selection from part two shapes itself like the lowering mountains and rocks, in craggy lines and darkening syntax.

IV The Melville story presents and defines its own reality, providing the evidence within itself to determine displacements, substitutions, and repressions; there is no need to invoke a private fantasy to discover references. Of course, it might be possible to discover the way this story refers to Melville's life, and even to come to an understanding of the problems the author confronted privately when the story was written. But psychoanalytic theory confronts a whole new set of analytical difficulties when the art and the life are taken as a whole, and it is to that possibility this section will be devoted.

Psychoanalytic theory has powers that other theories lack; one of them is the capacity to grapple with enactments as they participate in the lives of their creators and users. My emphasis upon the strength of the theory to interpret a story without reference to the writer of the story makes a claim that I regard as important in showing how much psychoanalytic theory of art can achieve. I did that in part to obviate the criticism directed against psychoanalytic interpretations of art, that they simply show everything to be a function of the artist's psychosexual conflict. The theory is not so circumscribed, nor need it always refer back to biographical material. Yet it can successfully and most interestingly use biographical material, and that allows us to realize a form of interpretation that is beginning now to be more and more exercised: the integration of enactments with the lives of those who created them. The success of that endeavor depends on plentiful documentation as well as on revelatory material in the objects themselves, as in the case of the Messerschmidt busts. Where there is information, psychoanalytic theory of art can bring about an important cultural enactment of its own, an object that I call the "art-life." Efforts in that direction have been made by George Painter, H. R. Graetz, J.-P. Sartre, Peter Gay, Meyer Schapiro, and others.[23] The art-life puts within our grasp a remarkable object in itself, an object closely related to, and in a sense that seems to me defensible, the descendents of Freud's case histories. If we think of the case histories, as I suggested above, as creations that have come to be cultural objects in their own right, linked to other cultural objects in the tradition of European enactments, then the art-life can be seen as a product of psychoanalytic theory in its ultimate interpretative capacity. While psychoanalytic theory provides interpretations of the sort I have been discussing above, it goes beyond interpretations of enactments to the creation of a new sort of cultural object that brings together, in a narration, the life and the achieved work of supremely gifted creators.

Thus in its own way the psychoanalytic theory as a representational method has contributed to the domain of enactments, first through the genre of the case history, and second by extension through the creation of the art-life. I believe, though this is speculation, that Freud was attempting to establish the art-life in his essay on Leonardo da Vinci, an essay that has caused the greatest dissatisfaction with psychoanalytic interpretations.[24] Freud wondered if Leonardo's paintings could in themselves tell us something about his psychosexual history. To answer the question, Freud made use of what he believed to be accurate autobiographical reports, but it turned out that he had relied upon misinformed sources. Despite the mistakes, the observations may yet lead to a reconstruction of Leonardo's art and life in an illuminating construction, provided the psychoanalytic interpretation takes the historical reality into account. The limitations of Freud's analysis started a debate between art historians and psychoanalysts not unlike that already presented at the beginning of this chapter.

The art historians argued that there is far too little in Freud's portrait of Leonardo to show how closely Leonardo's paintings resembled those of his contemporaries. The debate then turned on the question of how far the psychological elements and the stylistic elements could be distinguished in analyzing an individual painting. While this will always be a vexed question, the views that emerged are clear. Thus the art historian Meyer Schapiro has attacked Freud's essay on the grounds that historical accounts can be given for every one of the subjects to be found in the paintings, and that where special significance is given to a pictorial organization, such as that in "The Virgin and St. Anne," we can find other such pyramidal forms and like subjects. Hence to see a special psychological meaning in this one painting is to ignore its historical affinities with others by different artists.

Defending Freud's position, the psychoanalyst Kurt Eissler argues that whatever the historical facts may have been, one can always meaningfully ask the question "Why this rather than that?" What an artist chooses to present has a determination in his psychic disposition for which a psychological inquiry is appropriate. Faced with the task of painting the Virgin and St. Anne, Leonardo had several choices to make; we can then inquire into the choice he made and ask why he chose to do it this way rather than another way. Eissler is correct in arguing that the psychological question is always relevant; but the opportunity to answer it depends upon possessing a great deal of detailed information, and with the case of Leonardo we do not have enough.[25]

Once more it should be pointed out that there is a fundamental difference between the search for a causal relationship between an artist's psychosexual development and his art, and the effort to reconstitute a whole new object for our needs as cultural beings. The art-life is far more than a psychoanalysis of the artist; it must establish psychoanalytically properties of the object as a work of art in the total context of a life and a historical moment. It may be, indeed, that such an effort exceeds our capacities as workers in the human sciences, and that the product exceeds the bounds of a compassable object, but the effort is a development out of the psychoanalytic theory of art whose possibilities remain unexplored.

V The other side of the art-life is the totality of the experience of the witness, and there too we are moving to consolidate insights that psychoanalytic theory of art first discovered in some of Freud's essays, especially those in which he speculated upon the sources of the particular, powerful feelings we have in the presence of enactments. The analysis of affects helps us to understand the claims to truth on the part of enactments, and I shall close this chapter with a brief argument of how the affective and the cognitive work together in the experience we have with enactments.

Freud observed that narrative fictions produced two particular effects: one was a feeling of the uncanny, and the other a feeling of distancing, of alienation, from the fictional world that had been created in a story. Stories put the hearer–reader to a peculiar test: they are so obviously made up, not true, yet at the same time true. They have, in their unreality, a degree of reality that goes beyond mere everyday experience. In short, what we sometimes think of as "aesthetic experience" possess special characteristics that are hard to understand. There are seeming contradictions and paradoxes that run throughout our experience of narrative fictions. And upon these peculiarities Freud had some insightful things to say.

The outcome of our experience with narrative fictions is one of both belief and disbelief. Freud's speculations on these states of mind and feeling occur in two separate papers. In a letter written to Romain Rolland in 1937, Freud recounts an experience he had when visiting Athens, standing on the Acropolis, he thought, "By the evidence of my senses I am now standing on the Acropolis, but I cannot believe it."[26] Palpable contradictions of this sort occur in our experience now and then, and their peculiar force led Freud to suggest that they occur because of a reactivation in the present of a powerful past experience that persists as an unconscious memory. To the experience itself Freud gave the description *Entfremdungsgefühl*— alienation or derealization. There is a whole set of such feelings, and they are closely tied to the experiences we have with enactments. Freud brought them together as follows:

These phenomena are to be observed in two forms: the subject feels either that a piece of reality or that a piece of his own self is strange to him. In the latter case we speak of "depersonalizations"; derealizations and depersonalizations are intimately connected.[27]

Derealizations and depersonalizations are experiences resulting from the effort to "keep something out of us," and they are to be contrasted with experiences such as *déjà vu* in which we "seek to accept something as belonging to our ego." Both inclusions and expulsions are common ways of reacting to narrative fictions, and they are in psychoanalytic terms "defenses" which help us to keep something away from the ego, or to integrate something into the ego.

The experience on the Acropolis described by Freud ("It is real, yet I don't believe") has its obverse form in our experience with enactments of a representational kind: "The events I have witnessed are unreal, yet I believe them to be true." Belief, unbelief, disbelief are states of mind that relate to cultural objects along with a tremendously varied set of affects. We know, of course, that much given to us in enactments is not "true," that enactments are "fictions," yet they persuade us in mysterious ways so that we believe the descriptions as plausible, even when we would deny their reality. If we follow out the hypothesis Freud puts forward, we would try to explain our credulities in terms of unconscious memory, but that once again forces the aesthetic experience into the model of the clinical inquiry, and does not pay sufficient attention to the strategies, powers, and stylistic organizations of enactments. As my study of the Melville story shows, it is the organization of the object that controls, to a large extent, the inclusions and exclusions upon which our beliefs and disbeliefs rest. But they too are reflections of states of unconscious and conscious thought whose realizations can only occur in the presence of enactments. That is why the experience with enactments is at once affectively powerful and cognitively illuminating.

A useful supplement in the analysis of feelings entertained toward cultural objects, of which *Entfremdungsgefühl* is one sort, is provided by Freud's analysis of the experience of the uncanny in the essay with that title. In "The Uncanny" (*Das Unheimliche*) Freud proposed the view that feelings of the uncanny are induced by an event when it matches or confirms a thought, wish, fantasy that has been repressed. When that happens, it appears as if that which we feared or deeply desired is confirmed, and we think: "It is really true that such and such occurs." For example, we think, "It is really true that the dead come back to life; that mysterious magical forces pervade the universe," and the like. And in many narrative fictions, we conclude that we humans do possess extraordinary powers, or that we are capable of putting ourselves in touch with the past, or that we are doomed to tragic destruction, or that there are noumenal realities that can enter our lives, and so on and so on. In both real life and in fiction the uncanny is encountered. Freud's fascinating description of the contrast between the two encounters is very much to the point here:

The uncanny as it is depicted in *literature*, in stories and in imaginative productions, merits in truth a separate discussion. Above all, it is a much more fertile province than the uncanny in real life, for it contains the whole of the latter and something more besides, something that cannot be found in real life. The contrast between what has been repressed and what has been surmounted [Freud here is referring to beliefs that have been tested in real life and about which we have some empirical confirmation] cannot be transposed onto the uncanny in fiction without profound modification; for the realm of phantasy depends for its effect on the fact that its content is not submitted to reality-testing. The somewhat paradoxical result is that *in the first place a great deal that is not uncanny in fiction would be so if it happened in real life; and in the second place that there are many more means of creating uncanny effects in fiction than there are in real life.*[28]

Enactments of the sort I have been using as illustrations in this chapter demonstrate that indeed there are many more means of creating uncanny effects in fiction than there are in real life, for narrative fictions confirm the deeply held, often unconscious, beliefs about the external world of physical reality and the internal world of psychic reality. Thus the experience of the uncanny as we discover it in fiction establishes connections between our wishes and fantasies, and the further realms of physical and psychological reality which we reach by means of interpretative methods established by the sciences. But that is the assumption of the *scientific* inquirer attempting to confirm hypotheses about physical and psychic reality. Freud insisted throughout all his writings that in our everyday lives, and in our use of enactments, we make the inferential moves in deeply nonscientific ways, through affective means establishing those connections in terms of inner needs.

Needs for transportation to the realms beyond—seemingly realized in many experiences among which is the experience of the uncanny—are satisfied through fictional enactments which function for us as transitional objects in our accommodations to nature and to culture. Remarkable consequences follow from the power of enactments to function as transitional objects: dubious reality is given substance through indubitable fiction.

It is the cultural presence within us, established at a very early stage in our development, that determines our deepest beliefs and disbeliefs throughout our lives. If we are to pose the philosophical question about "reality," to determine its contours and its boundaries, we must answer in terms of things we create as much as through the natural world we inhabit, for "realities" exist within as well as without.

V

Psychoanalytic Theory
and Art History

I A psychoanalytic theory of art, presupposing the developmental forces in a life, and defining those forces in terms of their relationship to objects, projects the individual's involvement with culture as a lifelong interaction with objects. Yet individuals live in a history shared with others, participate in tradition, and add to tradition in their own conscious making. It has often been said that psychoanalytic theory—especially as a theory of art—ignores that which most fully fills our lives: history, the lived continuum of shared events. As I have repeatedly argued in the foregoing chapters, our developmental journey is historical in two senses: the psychological, and the world-historical; how then shall they be brought together? A philosophy of art dedicated to objects must, it would seem, concern itself with history.

A mournful observation occurs in one of Wittgenstein's notebook entries written while he was thinking out *Tractatus Logico-Philosophicus: Was geht mich die Geschichte an? Meine Welt ist die erste und einzige.* (What has history to do with me? Mine is the first and only world.)[1]

Wittgenstein's laconic rumination about self and history echoes Freud's general tendency to disregard history in the clinical setting, as if asking the question on behalf of the patient. Yet in so many ways history enters our private consciousness. And although "my world" may end with the end of my consciousness, I can hardly claim that my consciousness exhausts the world, or that there are no presences, realities, objects, and events that do not come into my consciousness from elsewhere, creating for me a distinct, ever-present awareness of mine and other, inner and outer, recollection and recognition.

When we ask Wittgenstein's anxiety-ridden question "What has history to do with me? Mine is the first and only world," we seek an answer that would justify our involvement with cultural objects, and the deep impact they have upon our lives. Does not my life and my world—however I construe them— include my unconscious as well as my conscious? Psychoanalytic theory insists that, of course, they all are compacted into one identity and yet also insists that the primary process is exempt from history. When we consider the ways our lives interfuse with objects, it would appear that it is not accurate to say, as Freud said, that the unconscious is outside of and indifferent to history. We certainly can conjecture that the unconscious is affected by history and subject to historical causation. The unconscious, after all, is not the "noumenal," an unknown, unknowable, yet logically necessary realm. Rather, the unconscious comes to be known through the process of interpretation. If we assert, as Wittgenstein did, that "the world" is first and only "my world," then we are indeed covering ourselves with the cloak of solipsism.

That solipsism threatens psychoanalytic theory in its isolating the unconscious seems obvious; and yet as a thoroughgoing developmentalism, the theory addresses itself to both persons and objects in their interrelationship. Freud's inclination to separate the self from history seems then to pose a contradiction for the theory and to deprive it of its necessary reference to the external reality of world and tradition. There is danger in Freud's isolation of the unconscious, as there is in Wittgenstein's insistence upon "my world" as the only world. The object-world is public, historically shared, cumulative in the ways objects reflect and influence one another, so that a theory of objects ought to address the historical and the private in their interdependence.

Despite Freud's denial that there is a historical dimension in the unconscious, our relationship to enactments—as we know it for ourselves, as we reconstruct it for others in the past— suggests there is a historical aspect of the unconscious, and that one way we might come to grasp a history of the unconscious, if we can begin to think that way, is through the study of enactments. Art history, I maintain, has an important contribution to make to the theory of psychic life. A psychoanalytic theory of art cannot be indifferent to the discoveries and methods of art history as it has grown up in the last two centuries; indeed, part of its coming into investigative power is due to the ways in which psychoanalytic theory of art and strict historical study have influenced one another.

In one respect Freud's theory took into account the ways individuals and objects interact; his investigations on narcissism concluded that every ego-ideal has a social as well as an individual side to it, and that formation of conscience is attached to many kinds of objects, among which I would include enactments. Freud always tended to see enactments as mirrors of theory, rather than as forces in the social and political world that help to shape the content of both primary process and secondary process thinking. Internalization of objects is an essential part of the developmental process. What has not been recognized is the metaphoric power of the *internalization of one object by another object.* Through imitation, quotation, stylistic repetition and affinity; through iconographic similarity, repetition of forms and reaffirmation of *topoi*, objects in the tradition of enactments stand to one another as "ego-ideals." Interrelationships of objects in history is analogous to, functions as a metaphor of, the responsive interaction of persons and objects. By analogy we come to see ourselves as possessing a world into which many other worlds have penetrated. The ultimate shape of "my world" integrates other worlds; so that if I ask, "What has history to do with me?" the answer is, the "me" I ask about is known in and through objects that possess in themselves many identities which become part of my identity.

"What has history to do with me?" has a coordinate question to be put in the realm of objects: "What have objects, like works of art, to do with the world?" Just as I might regard myself as insulated from history, so I might regard objects, once made, as free from and indifferent to the world. The psychosocial history of the person, and the style-art history of the object, can be described and understood only in terms of a world that stands opposed to self and object, as it is the world in which self and object function. Thus we are coerced by reality to think of ourselves as private consciousnesses that live in the world; and we can, by analogy, think of the enactments we produce as in a great variety of ways possessing the world that gives them referential possibilities. Objects must remain part of the world if they are to survive through generations; loss of the world entails loss of recognition. The world objects refer to includes the consciousnesses that make the objects, and the objects include in our understanding of them past consciousnesses that responded to them.

Enactments possess a complexity of structure and location that makes historical and psychoanalytic reconstruction and reconstitution a constant task, and I think of that activity in terms of a cultural product of a special kind to which I have given the name the "art-life." Indeed, it may be that we today have a greater interest than did earlier generations in the totality of the artist and the artist's works in their totality, as products of an interpretative effort requiring the contributions of several theories. The contribution of psychoanalytic theory to the establishment of the art-life seems to me essential, for it provides a method to recover repressed material. As the method is extended beyond the clinical to the cultural, it points to ways in which the objects may be reconstituted, even reconstructed where a great deal may be at first unavailable. Repressed, latent material may be fitted into its proper place in the process of recovery that interpretation makes possible. Perhaps because of its preoccupation with language, psychoanalytic interpretation has contributed in the most illuminating way to linguistic objects. Of linguistic objects, poetry builds upon condensation and displacement most powerfully, so that an example drawn from poetry may best illustrate the several inferential moves that lead to making the object whole.[2]

In any interpretation the question of an appropriate boundary for the inferential moves is pertinent, and sometimes difficult to establish. There is no doubt that conceptions of boundary are themselves historical events whose understanding requires both art-historical and psychoanalytic accounts, but they may not be coincident in their aims, though they are always relevant to one another. In the following interpretation, addressed to a set of poems by Emily Dickinson, I shall describe and execute some of the inferences that contribute, at least partially, to a reconstitution of meaning.

Previous discussions of poem 1146 by Emily Dickinson, which was the first of the volcano poems to be analyzed for syntactic deletions, led to the observation that the line "Than when she shows her Garnet Tooth" is incomplete in the sense that from a suspected compression we can postulate a deletion. The verb suggested to complete the assumed comparison was "roars," taking it as the fourth, missing, term in the following: "basks" is to "purrs" as "shows her Garnet Tooth" is to a missing verb; in this case, it was conjectured to be "roars."[3] Analyses of this kind assume both stylistic and linguistic criteria based upon traditions that it is the business of art history to discover. My supplementary analysis assumes that larger issues of meaning are involved, and that the psychoanalytic techniques for recovery of meaning will be helpful in understanding not only the individual poem 1146 but also its companion poems, by the same author, which develop the volcano themes.

1146

When Etna basks and purrs
Naples is more afraid
Than when she shows her Garnet Tooth—
Security is loud—[4]

The following thoughts underly the opening line of the poem:

1. Cats bask and purr.
2. Basking and purring cats are in a state of relaxed readiness.
3. One volcano state is that of relaxed readiness.
4. Therefore, a basking-purring cat is like a quiescent volcano, and a quiescent volcano is like a basking-purring cat.

A similar analysis applied to line three yields:

5. An erupting volcano is like an angry cat.
6. Cats bare a tooth when angry.
7. Therefore, eruption is like fang-baring.
8. The mouth of an animal is red.
9. Erupting volcanoes spew forth red lava from a fiery opening.
10. Therefore, the bared tooth can be described as red (Garnet).

By a process of analysis through immediate inference the above conditions underlying the assertions have been made explicit. But they are only the foundation for the inferences that the poem imposes upon us and that we are obliged to make if we want to understand what is said. Thus it is appropriate to ask, "What is the meaning of the poem," and to answer making and following inferences. Doing that brings us to interesting though somewhat puzzling thoughts.

Residents of Naples would quite rightly be afraid if a volcano erupted or threatened to erupt nearby. However, we should observe with a sense of slight bafflement, Etna is a volcano in Sicily; the volcano near Naples is Vesuvius. That the poet knew her geography well, and that the juxtaposition of Etna and Naples is no accident, we can confirm from Emily Dickinson's letters. Some readers, among whom I would count strict formalist theoreticians of our time, would object to my referring to beliefs of the poet expressed in other documents. But I think a reader might well ponder the likelihood of the poem being factually mistaken—that is, that the poem asserts the belief that Etna and Naples are contiguous, and therefore the poem makes a serious mistake. If so, the inferences the poem demands of us are of one sort; while they are of a different sort if we assume, on whatever evidence—including the evidence of poetic meaningfulness in an ultimate sense—that the poem intends to juxtapose two places geographically distant from one another.

Why should the behavior of Etna arouse fear in the residents of Naples? Is the security of Neapolitans threatened by the noise of Etna erupting? If so, how are the two events related? "Security is loud—" implies that when Etna erupts Neapolitans hear it and feel secure.

As we read the poem and ponder its assertions, we are very likely to formulate hypotheses, three of which might be the following:

i. *Geological hypothesis.* The inhabitants of Naples live near a volcano, Vesuvius. They have observed that when the distant volcano, Etna, is quiescent, their nearby volcano is apt to erupt; the state of Etna is inversely related to the state of Vesuvius. When Etna does erupt, Neapolitans are relieved, and because their security is a function of Etna's condition, to say "Security is loud—" suggests that when Etna erupts Neapolitans hear it, and find security in knowing Vesuvius will not erupt at that time.

ii. *Psychological hypothesis.* If we are familiar with other poems by Emily Dickinson, we would be likely to formulate another hypothesis. Poem 1146 can be understood to describe relationships between people, in the following sense: the two conditions of Etna, quiescent and eruptive, refer to states of human beings. On this hypothesis, we would attempt to recover from the poem a theory about people and their psychological states. Geological descriptions are, as it were, the surface structures, beneath which, through a series of transformations, we may uncover descriptions of emotions, beliefs, and dispositions. Indeed, it may be that the poem itself represents a process of transformation for the volcano hides something we must find, and the poem hides something we are elicited to seek. Putting forth the hypotheses is an act of recovery, an attempt to dig deeper in both the literal and figurative sense. But to do that, we require further information to guide us, and therefore, once more, we must move beyond the language of poem 1146 to other poems by Emily Dickinson.

III. *Influence hypothesis.* The ideas in the poem do not seem unusual or remote; in fact, they have a certain topological commonness, for the interest in buried cities and in the volcanoes of Italy and Sicily was widespread in transcendentalist New England. One evidence of this, and a possible source for Emily Dickinson's ruminations on volcanoes, is the following passage from R. W. Emerson's famous Phi Beta Kappa lecture of 1837, entitled "The American Scholar." A deeply felt, quasi-religious attribution of the gratification to be found in scholarship of the past culminates in words that Emily Dickinson put to a poetic use far from Emerson's somewhat banal spirituality:

The man has never lived that can feed us ever. The human mind cannot be enshrined in a person who shall set a barrier on any one side to this unbounded, unboundable empire. It is one central fire, which, flaming now out of the lips of Etna, lightens the capes of Sicily, and now out of the throat of Vesuvius, illuminates the towers and vineyards of Naples. It is one light which beams out of a thousand stars. It is one soul which animates all men.[5]

To what a vast difference of interpretation the poet put those words! To follow out all their implications the methods and interpretative strategies of psychoanalytic theory will help. When influence is discovered, meaning does not follow with clear assurance of continuity. The same words undergo deep transformation in a new context.

In the manner of old-fashioned logic textbooks, we might now distinguish immediate and mediate inferences; the first having been given in 1–10 above, and the second in I, II, and III; but I, II, and III would not be proposed were it not for 1–10. Notice that 1–10 are inferential moves that can be made from the sentences of the poem itself, while I, II, and III can be made only by inferential moves that carry us far beyond the evidence immediately available. As we move farther from the sentences of the poem, poems on similar subjects become interesting; let us consider some of them. Poem 175 compares the human face to volcanic stillness; 601 adds an enlightening comparison: "A quiet—Earthquake Style—/Too subtle to suspect" refers to a district distant from Naples that cannot detect volcanic events in the vicinity of Naples. The volcano is said to be explicitly a "Symbol," powerful enough to annihilate cities. Its method of destruction is part human, part monster "Whose hissing Corals part—and shut—/And Cities—ooze away—. Finally, 754 draws together a set of interrelated thoughts that connect eruption to human pleasure, for "It is as a Vesuvian face/Had let its pleasure through—." By adding information from 1677 we can make the necessary inferences demanded by 1146. I suggest the following as a first approximate filling out of the argument:

Naples' neighbor, Vesuvius, though geographically near, is not a threat. The real threat is the geographically distant, but psychologically near, Etna. The shift from geography to psychology suggests that the volcanic condition we fear and respond to is that of the self or person; and its threat can only be gauged by the person through an awareness of private eruptive threats, and by analogy to the explosive behavior of others. We harbor aggressive anger, apt to erupt; and our quiescent states only seem so. Thus those living in Naples (metaphorically speaking) relate their own inner pent-up force and potential destructiveness to the distant Etna. Volcanic destruction then refers to the aggressive anger of persons who must learn to gauge forces within themselves and forces destructively turned toward them from without.

"Security is loud—" now begins to take on meaning through an analogy: volcanoes are like people; when persons erupt they achieve pleasure; when they are quiescent they suffer. Eruptions give "security" in two senses: to the one erupting they give gratification; to the one distant and afraid of aggression coming from without, they reveal the true state of affairs, and so, at least for the moment, one can feel secure, for the explosion is visible, the aggression manifest. Once it sinks again into latency, one lives in fear of a recurrence.

Latency in emotional states is matched to the latency of the poem itself, which suppresses or keeps under the pressure of feeling the force of anger and of meaning waiting to realize and assert itself. The poem is, analogously, a volcano, as a person is, analogously, a volcano. Poem and person are closely related. How that comes about I shall return to below.

The strategies of containment, revelation, shifting of meaning, repression, contamination of related thought through repression—all of the mechanisms and forces psychoanalytic theory is built upon—are demonstrated in this brief poem. Its very conclusion has demanded the formulation of hypotheses in order to relate it to the world of which it is a part, and that world now has taken shape in terms of its psychological, geographical, and artistic structures. Those relationships—leading so far away from the manifest content of the poem—have been presented as ideas, rather abstract and remote, far removed from the specific references of the poems that here form an interrelated cluster. As psychoanalytic interpretation insists, meanings emerge from compression of both words and objects.

Almost all of the objects whose images occur in the poems can be reconstructed from the most complex volcano poem— that is, 754. In the set of volcano poems, there is a puzzling collocation of things, such as "Garnet Tooth," "hissing Corals,"

"How red the Fire rocks below—" "Grass," "Bird" on one side; geographical terms and abstract religious terms such as "Resumption Morn" and "Immortality" on the other side. Objects, persons, and the life to come all intersect in these poems. Their deeper implications have yet to come into focus. Through 754 the deep interconnection of aggressive destructiveness and the hope for and possibility assigned to a state beyond death— immortality—begins to emerge. And along with that interconnection, the poem begins to demonstrate the ways in which poems and people are alike one another. Metaphors state the relationships, first in "Vesuvian face" and second in the concluding stanza, which asserts the difference between killing and dying.

The final metaphor identifies the poet and the poet's making as split between the killing force and the surviving spirit; to be a poet requires realization of both. Poets are volcanoes, we can say, putting it very crudely and really inappropriately for the subtlety of these poems. As poets they are creators in several senses that include, along with destruction and survival, a deep sexuality that goes beyond sex to the sexualization of the force of creativity itself. It is not irrelevant, in the context of these identifications, to know and to remark that the poet is a woman.

The sexuality of the poems, again, is summed up in 754, whose narrative describes a total life, a life of creativity, of passionate attachment, of failure and success in both love and creativity. The reflections of the themes through one another project a complex image that now can begin to come into focus; it is an image that includes the person of the poet (of which I will have more to say below) and the nature of poetic sexuality, and the ways natural objects (volcanoes) and a woman writing about volcanoes reflect one another. Volcanoes are persons; persons are volcanoes. Most appropriately, women seize the volcano as the sexualized object because it asserts many aspects of female sexual feeling. The poet has found, partly through the spirituality of Emerson, her own physical and spiritualized sexuality. It is a wonderful irony of historical interaction that the Phi Beta Kappa address should have such erotically energetic consequences. But then, can sages control the violence of volcanic longings? Even the historical accident of the repressed Boston transcendentalist speaking to and through a poet, a woman, who is able to lift the repression, has its antecedents in repetitions of the classical past. Perhaps Emily Dickinson even recognized that deepest of all historical affinities: that she realized a sublimation (in the artistic sense) of a classical conflict between male repression and female capacity to raise the latent into the manifest, if only there were witnesses to echo the volcanic ordnance she set off.

But how, then, shall we see the poet in the poems? It has become popular today to speak of "poetic personae" in the belief that by so doing we can overcome an epistemological problem. Critics and philosophers have tended to duplicate in analyses of literary art the problems they have inherited from modern epistemology. As we cannot decide how we are related to the external world of natural events, so we cannot decide how we are related to the literary world of imagined events. In both cases we are filled with anxieties about failing to get through to "reality." In our despair at failure to encounter the natural world we have, once upon a time, created "sense data"; in our uncertainties about whether or not we can know the "reality" of the poet we still create "personae."

Pondering the volcano poems of Emily Dickinson, it seems to me that a reversal of the identification is more apt and truer to the realities we deal with in literary language: Emily Dickinson is the persona of her poems, rather than the poems being personae of the poet, Emily Dickinson.

The poems are received by us as the speaking voice of a person, a person we know about historically, to some extent, and a person we can get to know exhaustively, poetically, *as a poet*. The poems are not masks—whether penetrable or impenetrable—but realities we know with increasing fullness and complexity as we hear and re-hear, read and re-read them. As persons, they speak totally co-extensively with their own intentions. They themselves are as deep as any person, and take longer to know than any person we can know, for they are known by generations of reflecting minds who respond to them. They might, in some sense, come to be fully explored, which is not possible with a living person.

This fundamental difference between poems and persons comes out clearly in our consideration of the volcano poems of Emily Dickinson. As objects, constituting part of a tradition, poems are subjected to an analysis that endures through time. Now curiously enough we can, and at the present time do, have an analogous situation with interpretations that have come down to us, much as if they were enactments. I refer to the interpretations that are embedded in Freud's major inquiry, *The Interpretation of Dreams*. That work has been subjected to continuous reinterpretation since the author gave the original interpretations of the dreams he dreamt. That places the examples in the same relative situation as enactments. We are now reconsidering the dreams in the light of later material, essentially historical material, that Freud himself did not have access to, or was completely unconscious of.

The interpretations offered by psychoanalytic theory of art also reintroduce objects for consideration in the historical context. Part of history is exactly the history of persons; they have lives that fasten them to the historical in the largest sense beyond their private psychosexual histories. And in psychoanalytic interpretation the private is a mask through which the enduring objects can be discovered. The psychosexual history can be likened to a mask through which we penetrate to get to reality. So, analogously, the poet is a mask through which we shall find the poems. But the creation of the mask occurs as the poems unfold. Thus the process of "personification" in psychoanalytic theory is just the opposite of what it has been taken to be. The correct psychoanalytic method with enactments is to begin with the objects; they are the reality. After prolonged—perhaps continuing over generations—interpretation and analysis of the objects, a persona emerges: the poet. It is a mistake to accuse the psychoanalytic of reducing everything to biography as if that is a necessary part of the method. Although that mistake has often been made, the interesting and constructive use of psychoanalytic method is to begin with the objects, where the focus of interpretation is enactments. Then, from careful and sustained interpretation, the reality of objects yields the mask of the poet.

The poet recognizes this as the true order of revelation. Poem 754 explains the intricacies of the relationship between poet and poem. The poet, as any person, possesses a life and a creative will. The creative force produces the poem, which is immortal and lives on; the life dies. Yet life is conceived as a "Loaded Gun," waiting to find its prey and its hunter. The creative self comes to be the agent of destruction and of construction. To produce the immortal object, tremendous aggressive, destructive force must be expended. And after such expenditure, the life ceases. But the power to die is, paradoxically, the power to achieve eternal life as an eternal object, the poem that survives. The poet dies; the poem lives. And *it* is that life we possess. It is the reality, and at best the poet is but a mask, necessarily self-effacing. The constituents of the mask are metaphorically spoken: "Loaded Gun," "Vesuvian face," "Yellow Eye," "emphatic Thumb." They are like the topological, facial physiognomy of the mask: extreme, almost caricature, organs of expression and destruction. They make the kill, but not the resurrected object: "Resumption Morn" is in the bag of the hunt, the poems we possess. And we too must go after the poems as hunters, with the same aggressive force and possibility, if we know how, of establishing the immortal object.

II We can begin to answer Wittgenstein's question. History has everything to do with me, for history *makes* my world, insofar as I have a world at all. *My* world, to be sure, is the only world I can know, but in coming to know my world I join in the larger historical world to which all consciousness attaches. Even if I were to limit "my world" to enactments, whose "reality" I might question, I can come to know my world only through the exploration of enactments, and they are necessarily shared objects. To possess a world at all, I must possess history, to the extent that, at the least, history is a set of cultural objects structured in a tradition. What history might be for me beyond that minimum depends upon accidents of growth and of position in the social reality. History makes *the* world of which *my* world is a part; only in sharing in the world do I realize myself as a participant in a tradition. As there can be no private language, so there can be no private world.

To say "Mine is the first and only world" is to take the position of the infant, starting out on the journey that carries from total immersion in the narcissistic phase of life, to the common possession of common objects. If we ask, "What has history to do with me?" the answer then is that the tradition of cultural objects establishes history in the first, most primitive, and most basic sense of "history." From the basic sense, history grows and expands to its full multidimensional complexity. The question then should be restated: "How is it I become what I am through the agency of history?" And the answer: "History endows me with the only enduring human reality." The first and only world is the only world I can possess.

"Possession of a world" brings the argument back to the comparison with which chapter 2 began. Natural philosophy, as represented by the Newtonian effort to explain nature, assumed that the only world to be possessed, to be in any meaningful sense of the word "a world," is the world of nature, the "external world" of traditional modern philosophy. Although Freud accepted that *Weltanschauung* as his own, his science established an alternative to the reality of the physical world: the reality of culture. The internal "world" of cultural reality is the only world I can possess in the meaningful sense of "possess." While I can explore, know, investigate, predict, and to some extent control the physical world, *my world* is the world of human objects—in short, of enactments. The world that I can come to possess and to express and to contribute to is the world of interrelated cultural objects that constitute a tradition. To possess a world requires that I enter it historically—that is, seize it as a set of interrelated, interinanimated objects that refer to one another as well as to me.

That the physical world maintains a fundamental dependence upon the tradition of cultural objects emerges from the example of the volcano poems. Possession of "the world," in the sense of the reality referred to by physical science, comes to realization in part at least through the objects we know as enactments. Fanciful and "false" as the observations on volcanoes made by Emily Dickinson may be from the point of view of geology, they are true statements about persons and objects in the deepest ways persons and object interrelate to one another. We cannot be said to know a language if we know only one word; so we cannot be said to know enactments if we are acquainted with one—or a few—of them. The interconnection of enactments is a condition for knowing one enactment.

And finally my world can only be "mine" when others share it; there can be no pure private experience. Nor can there be pure objects in the sense of objects known only by me, however much our fantasies assure us of the possibility of the purely private. That we entertain such fantasies becomes for us the distinguishing mark of our remoteness from reality. But now "reality" slips from us; we wonder what we can mean by "reality."

A consequence of psychoanalytic method is its insistence on the impossibility of solipsism, in either philosophy or psychology. Freud's therapeutic practice, and its method, cut through our fantasies of privacy as no other has done. The reality psychoanalysis puts us in touch with is the reality that gets articulated with the analytic process: the latent thought, whether in the clinic or in the tradition of enactments, becomes artistically efficacious when brought into consciousness, through the process of interpretation. Despite the fact that for Freud history is "case history," the reality that doctor and patient share is not drawn by the boundary of the consulting room. Their shared reality reaches far beyond the consulting room to the cultural history whose presence in and through objects makes possible the process and the outcome of the method. Object-thoughts have their particular stylistic manifestations, a representation of deep historical forces; and indeed it may be that dream-thoughts too possess stylistic individuality, and that the dreams of one time are not stylistically coherent with those of another. If primary process thinking is influenced by objects and by secondary process thinking, then dreams, like art, may have identifiable historical locations. But these speculations are merely suggestions for possible cultural inquiry; the central psychoanalytic insight that historical research can put to its own use is that with deepening self-consciousness, repression is lifted. The repressed then is integrated into the objects that art-historical study thinks about. As the thought goes on, through generations of reflection, the objects become revelatory of their own depths and the degree to which they represent other objects. As the repressed material manifests itself in objects, the historian possesses more and more to interpret. The hidden and unavailable becomes available for other varieties of explanation. What the psychoanalytic helps us to grasp is useful not only to the psychoanalytic; psychoanalytic discoveries can be used by investigators working in terms of other theories.

As Hegel saw, and as he led us to see, the historical process is forever churning up its own unconscious into consciousness. We come to learn of this unrelenting revelation particularly through the study of enactments in a tradition. In some contributing way, the art historian abets the churning, leading successive witnesses to seize more and more consciously that which before was unconscious and unavailable to consciousness. It is the historian together with the clinician-therapist who transforms the confined case history to the larger, and more readily accessible, object-history.

How the historical and psychoanalytic work together in the interpretation of objects may be stated in somewhat the following form. In one sense, all psychoanalytic interpretation is historical, in the sense that it investigates the history of the individual and it proposes a theory that describes and predicts developmental stages in the life trajectory. The question then for psychoanalytic theory and art history is this: Is there any place in psychoanalytic description for the historical in the nonpersonal sense of history as public process in which cultures themselves are caught up? The private aspect of the psychoanalytic does find a historical perspective in the larger scene, for the processes of repression, of object relationships, of neurosis and psychosis always take place in the world: *my* world is shaped by and is part of *the* world. My behavior occurs in the world and is responded to by the world, or a segment of it. My products—my actions, my objects, my thoughts insofar as I externalize them—exist in the world as events that others respond to. It is an artificial distinction to separate out from history that which is private behavior, or to identify one set of events as properly historical, and another as not. Enactments are historical events as much as are world wars and presidential elections. The aim of psychoanalytic interpretation is to focus on the object which affects us deeply, which is, as the theory says, highly cathected. Its representational powers are infinite, and it can be the cathected object whose content represents history in a variety of ways. It both participates in and represents events that are common to all. Thus the very object itself may be the occasion for the juncture of the psychological and the historical and the ways they do in fact interact.

My argument for the applicability of psychoanalytic theory

as an accompaniment to art history rests upon the fundamental and universal material psychoanalytic theory deals with: the developmental as such, the dynamic process of growing up which underlies and forces each individual to cope with objects in a dynamic, changing way throughout life. Each one of us, insofar as each one internalizes the tradition—whether inherited or willfully mapped anew—lives an art-life whose totality will always resemble, in respects more or less original, the exemplary cases that artists create. Psychoanalytic theory embodies within itself a conception of the art-life which has been illustrated by the many examples of this inquiry. In its own contribution to the art-life, psychoanalysis added to the historical idealism of Hegel a deeper understanding of maturational possibilities each one of us might realize. And it was at this juncture our inquiry began.

Now that it is at an end, I seek to emphasize the complementary contributions of the historical and the psychological. Art history, dwelling as it usually does upon the evolutionary trajectory of forms, has tended to slight the object in its other relationships: to the artist and to the perceiver. The psychological, in its psychoanalytic mode, realizes precisely the cases we need for objects in their relationships to persons. That too is part of history, and it is that part of history which the psychoanalytic can most usefully inform.

A further benefit follows from the psychoanalytic theory of art, a benefit close to that realized by philosophy when it truly enlightens us. Psychoanalysis was addressed to the cure of mental illness; it was originally conceived as a therapy, and only incidentally as a theory of culture. But its applicability to culture was early recognized by Freud, and that strand has been woven through much subsequent psychoanalytic speculation. The therapeutic powers of psychoanalysis are evident in its cultural applications as well. For the psychoanalytic theory of culture relieves delusions that can be inhibiting and even dangerous to our health as cultural beings. In reviewing the assumptions and conduct of the past, it calls us back to the humane, to that we as possessors of a tradition need to remember of the tradition and its genesis, its continuity, its recurrent values.

As Emily Dickinson forces us to recognize, the one life granted to each of us offers the choice: dedication to killing, or to dying. Traditionally it was thought to be a benefit conferred by philosophy that somehow or other to philosophize is to learn how to die. Perhaps even now that belief is not idle, if it attaches to exercises no longer declared to be philosophical, the reflections we are compelled to entertain on witnessing *King Lear*. And yet we need not have the spur of that particular enactment to have the Vesuvian pleasures the hunt brings home. It is the dedication to the hunt that makes the life, both in its creative achievements and in its final assessment of itself. In these pursuits psychoanalytic theory of culture reminds us of the things we ought to value, for, coming as it did out of the philosophically mature, thoughtful contributions of the modern tradition, it has worked to make available the best that our tradition has been able to conceive, not in the direction of the natural sciences it mistakenly took itself to be furthering, but in the human sciences of which it now forms a fundamental part.

Appendix

Poems of Emily Dickinson referred to above:

175

I have never seen 'Volcanoes'—
But when Travellers tell
How those old—phlegmatic mountains
Usually so still—

Bear within—appalling Ordnance,
Fire, and smoke, and gun,
Taking Villages for breakfast,
And appalling Men—

If the stillness is Volcanic
In the human face
When upon a pain Titanic
Features keep their place—

If at length the smouldering anguish
Will not overcome—
And the palpitating Vineyard
In the dust, be thrown?

If some loving Antiquary,
On Resumption Morn,
Will not cry with joy 'Pompeii'!
To the Hills return!

601

A still—Volcano—Life—
That flickered in the night—
When it was dark enough to do
Without erasing sight—

A quiet—Earthquake Style—
Too subtle to suspect
By natures this side Naples—
The North cannot detect

The Solemn—Torrid—Symbol—
The lips that never lie—
Whose hissing Corals part—and shut—
And cities—ooze away—

754

My Life had stood—a Loaded Gun—
In Corners—till a Day
The Owner passed—identified—
And carried Me away—

And now We roam in Sovereign Woods—
And now We hunt the Doe—
And every time I speak for Him—
The Mountains straight reply—

And do I smile, such cordial light
Upon the Valley glow—
It is as a Vesuvian face
Had let its pleasure through—

And when at Night—Our good Day done—
I guard My Master's Head—
'Tis better than the Eider-Duck's
Deep Pillow—to have shared—

To foe of His—I'm deadly foe—
None stir the second time—
On whom I lay a Yellow Eye—
Or an emphatic Thumb—

Though I than He—may longer live
He longer must—than I—
For I have but the power to kill,
Without—the power to die—

1146

When Etna basks and purrs
Naples is more afraid

Than when she shows her Garnet Tooth—
Security is loud—

1677

On my volcano grows the Grass
A meditative spot—
An acre for a Bird to choose
Would be the General thought—

How red the Fire rocks below—
How insecure the sod
Did I disclose
Would populate with awe my solitude.

1705

Volcanoes be in Sicily
And South America
I judge from my Geography—
Volcanoes nearer here
A Lava step at any time
Am I inclined to climb—
A Crater I may contemplate
Vesuvius at Home.

1748

The reticent volcano keeps
His never slumbering plan—
Confided are his projects pink
To no precarious man.

If nature will not tell the tale
Jehovah told to her
Can human nature not survive
Without a listener?

Admonished by her buckled lips
Let every babbler be
The only secret people keep
Is Immortality.

Notes

1. Introduction: The Place of Psychoanalytic Theory in Philosophy of Art

1. On Freud's style, see Peter Gay, "Sigmund Freud: A German and His Discontents," in *Freud, Jews, and Other Germans,* esp. pp. 50–52.

2. See Karl Mannheim, "On the Interpretation of Weltanschauung." For Freud's thought on the problem of *Weltanschauung,* see Lecture 35, "The Question of a Weltanschauung," *New Introductory Lectures on Psychoanalysis,* Std. Ed, 22:158–182. The question is taken up again, p. 41. The problem in art history is discussed by Ernst Gombrich, "The Logic of Vanity Fair."

3. *The Origins of Psychoanalysis.* See letter 71.

4. G. W. F. Hegel, *Vorlesungen über die Ästhetik.*

5. See the *Ästhetik,* part II, section III, ch. III, paragraph 3.

2. The Structure of the Theory for a Philosophy of Art

1. *Interpretation of Dreams,* Std. Ed., 4:145.

2. Std. Ed., 5:611.

3. *Ibid.,* p. 612.

4. Std. Ed., 5:612–613. Italics in original.

5. Std. Ed., 5:506–507, footnote added to edition of 1925.

6. Std. Ed., 5:506.

7. *Ibid.,* p. 507.

8. See Merton M. Gill, *Analysis of Transference,* vol. 1, "Theory and Technique" (New York: International Universities Press, 1982).

9. Compare, for example, the early paper "Creative Writers and Day-Dreaming," Std. Ed., 9:141–154, and *Moses and Monotheism,* Std. Ed., 23:7–140.

10. "Repression," Std. Ed., 14:148.

11. An effort to reconstruct early experiences can be found in Martha Wolfenstein, "The Image of the Lost Parent."

12. "On the History of the Psychoanalytic Movement," Std. Ed., 14:6.

13. Std. Ed., 14:141–158, p. 146.

14. Std. Ed., 19:235–239, p. 236.

15. Std. Ed., vol. 14, esp. pp. 149–150.

16. "An Outline of Psycho-Analysis," Std. Ed., 23:164.

17. A further account of primary and secondary process thinking may be found in the essay of 1915 "The Unconscious." Std. Ed., 14:186–187 especially. I have included this passage in an appendix to this chapter.

18. "An Autobiographical Study," Std. Ed., 20:72.

3. Psychoanalytic Theory of Culture

1. From "The Location of Cultural Experience," where Winnicott quotes himself. *International Journal of Psychoanalysis* (1966) 48:368.

2. Std. Ed., 22:158.

3. *Totem and Taboo,* Std. Ed., 13:90.

4. See esp. *Three Essays on the Theory of Sexuality,* Std. Ed., vol. 14.

5. "On Narcissism," Std. Ed., 14:101–102.

6. The class of enactments includes thought as well as the more obvious cultural objects. Thus, philosophical systems, theories of nature, society, culture, and so too psychoanalytic theory must be included in enactments. The implications of this inclusiveness are central to philosophy itself, for philosophy as containing a theory of enactments both presents and represents itself. This may be the distinguishing characteristic of philosophy as an enactment, and it serves to state the theory of which it itself is an instance.

7. The use of "transitional" refers to the thought of D. W. Winnicott, to be further discussed, pp. 59–64.

8. *Ego Psychology and the Problem of Adaptation,* Heinz Hartmann, p. 76.

9. *Ibid.,* p. 77.

10. Winnicott, "The Location of Cultural Experience," pp. 368ff.

11. *Ibid.,* pp. 370–371. Italics in original.

12. Roy Schafer, *Aspects of Internalization,* p. 225. Schafer notes also that among representations the most important are *self*-representations. We can observe the great many ways transitional objects serve as part of the child's identification, and also the degree to which there is "an unshakable libidinal attachment to . . . self-representations" (p. 255).

13. "The Dynamic Unconscious and the Self," unpublished paper, quoted with permission of Otto Kernberg.

14. *Ibid.*

15. *Ibid.*

16. *Ibid.*

17. Adrian Stokes, "The Luxury and Necessity of Painting," in *Three Essays on the Painting of Our Time,* pp. 10–11.

18. Maurice Merleau-Ponty, "The Metaphysical in Man," in *Sense and Non-*

Sense, Hubert L. Dreyfus and Patricia Allen Dreyfus, trans. (Evanston, Ill.: Northwestern University Press, 1964), p. 94.

19. "The Economic Problem of Masochism," Std. Ed., 19:168.

20. See my essay "Modernity and Death" in *Structures of Experience*, pp. 177–214; also, "The Beautiful and the Sublime."

21. D. W. Winnicott, "Communicating and Not Communicating Leading to a Study of Certain Opposites," in *The Maturational Processes and the Facilitating Environment*, p. 187. Italics in original.

22. Anna Freud, *The Ego and the Mechanisms of Defense* (New York: International Universities Press, 1946), p. 178.

23. Hartmann, *Ego Psychology*, p. 58.

24. *Ibid.*, pp. 72.

25. *Ibid.*, pp. 77–78.

4. Psychoanalytic Theory at Work: Style, Expression, Truth

1. Ernst Kris, *Psychoanalytic Explorations in Art*, ch. 4, "A Psychotic Sculptor of the Eighteenth Century," pp. 128–150, esp. pp. 147–148. Rudolf and Margot Wittkower, *Born Under Saturn* (New York: Norton, 1963), pp. 124–132.

2. See above, chapter 2, pp. 26–27. I have discussed the concept of "iconography of the medium" in "Semantics for Literary Languages," *New Literary History* (1972), no. 1, 4:91–106.

3. Rudolf and Margot Wittkower, *Born Under Saturn*, p. 129.

4. For these clinical observations see the essay "The Unconscious," Std. Ed., 14:159–216; and *The Interpretation of Dreams*, Std. Ed., ch. VII, Section (F).

5. Boccioni from "Preface, The First Exhibition of Futurist Sculpture," in Robert L. Herbert, ed., *Modern Artists on Art* (Englewood Cliffs, N.J.: Prentice-Hall, 1964), p. 55.

6. Norman Holland, *Psychoanalysis and Shakespeare*, pp. 31–32.

7. *Interpretation of Dreams*, Std. Ed. 4:101–102. Italics in original.

8. *The Moses of Michelangelo*, Std. Ed., 13:222.

9. A good example of attention to the obvious yet mysterious is Martha Wolfenstein's study of Magritte's painting. "The Image of the Lost Parent," pp. 444–455. The recurring pictorial ambiguity and mysteriousness of Magritte's art forces us to seek a coherent fantasy system to explain the surrealistic compositions. Wolfenstein analyzes the paintings into themes of presence–absence and life–death, and relates the preoccupation with dualities to an effort to cope with melancholia following the loss of a parent. The paintings as such are obviously concerned with properly painterly problems: appearance– reality, the interpenetration of past–present through memory, and so on. But in addition to that, the paintings are deeply private and personal; and that presence is explained by reference first to general clinical findings, and then to Magritte's own suffering as a child through the loss of his mother.

10. Std. Ed., 12:289–302.

11. For a further discussion of this theme in modern literature, see my "Modernity and Death: *The Leopard* of Lampedusa," in *Structures of Experience* also *Literature and Philosophy* (London: Routledge and Kegan Paul, 1971).

12. For further discussion of this point, see Paul Ricoeur, *Freud and Philosophy*. See also Freud, *Delusion and Dreams in Jensen's Gradiva*, Std. Ed., 9:1–95; GW, 7:31–125. Important discussions are to be found in "Psychopathische Personen auf der Bühne," Std. Ed., 17:305; and "The Loss of Reality in Neurosis and Psychosis," Std. Ed., 19:183–190.

13. On the political implications of Lear's division of the kingdom, see Allan Bloom, *Shakespeare's Politics* (with Harry V. Jaffa) (New York: Basic Books, 1964). I am indebted to this discussion for political points made here.

14. Std. Ed., 21:86.

15. *Ibid.*, p. 142.

16. See my discussion in *The House, the City, and the Judge*, ch. 5.

17. For Winnicott's speculations on cultural objects, see "The Location of Cultural Experience," *International Journal of Psycho-Analysis* (1966), 48:368–372.

18. Std. Ed., 23:195–204, 271–278.

19. "An Outline of Psychoanalysis," pp. 202–204.

20. "Splitting of the Ego," pp. 275–277.

21. See "From the History of an Infantile Neurosis," Std. Ed., vol. 17; and "The Loss of Reality in Neurosis and Psychosis," Std. Ed., vol. 19.

22. "The Loss of Reality," p. 187. Italics in original.

23. See Peter Gay, *Art and Act*; H. R. Graetz, *The Symbolic Language of Vincent Van Gogh*; George Painter, *Proust*; J.-P. Sartre, *L'Idiot de la famille*; Meyer Schapiro, "The Apples of Cézanne."

24. *Leonardo da Vinci and a Memory of His Childhood*, Std. Ed., 11:57–137.

25. See Meyer Schapiro, "Leonardo and Freud." See also K. R. Eissler, *Leonardo da Vinci*.

26. "A Disturbance of Memory on the Acropolis," Std. Ed., 22:243.

27. *Ibid.*, p. 245.

28. "The Uncanny," Std. Ed., 17:249. Italics in original.

5. Psychoanalytic Theory and Art History

1. Ludwig Wittgenstein, *Notebooks 1914–1916* (New York: Harper Torchbooks, 1969), p. 82.

2. See the discussion of this attempt at the recovery of meaning in my "Deletion and Compression in Poetry." Reference is made there to the source of the technique for discovering the material we might think of as "repressed." The discussion here in chapter 5 is an elaboration on this dispute.

3. The discussion occurs in S. Levin, "The Analysis of Compression in Poetry," *Foundations of Language* (1971), 7:38–55.

4. Emily Dickinson, *The Complete Poems of Emily Dickinson*, Thomas H. Johnson, ed. (Boston: Little, Brown, 1960), p. 513. See appendix, chapter 5, for the poems referred to.

5. *The Complete Essays and Other Writings of Ralph Waldo Emerson*, Brooks Atkinson, ed. (New York: Modern Library, 1940), p. 59.

Bibliography

Barthes, Roland. *S/Z*. New York: Hill and Wang, 1974.

Bowie, Theodore and Cornelia Christenson. *Studies in Erotic Art*. New York: Basic Books, 1970.

Brenner, Charles. *An Elementary Textbook of Psychoanalysis*. New York: Anchor Books, 1973.

Brown, Norman O. *Life Against Death: The Psychoanalytic Meaning of History*. Middletown, Conn.: Wesleyan University Press, 1959.

Carrier, David. "Adrian Stokes and the Theory of Painting." *British Journal of Aesthetics* (1973), 13:133–145.

Chasseguet-Smirgel, Janine. *Pour une psychoanalyse de l'art et de créativité*. Paris: Payot, 1971.

Cixous, Hélène. "Fiction and Its Phantoms: A Reading of Freud's *Das Unheimliche* ("The Uncanny"). *New Literary History* (1976), 7:525–548.

Cody, John. *After Great Pain: The Inner Life of Emily Dickinson*. Cambridge, Mass.: Harvard University Press, 1971.

Dalton, Elizabeth. *Unconscious Structure in the Idiot: A Study in Literature and Psychoanalysis*. Princeton: Princeton University Press, 1978.

Derrida, Jacques. *De la grammatologie*. Paris: Edition de Minuit, 1967. English trans. by G. C. Spivak. Baltimore: Johns Hopkins University Press, 1976.

—— *Écriture et la différence*. Paris: Editions du Seuil, 1967.

Douglas, Mary. *Purity and Danger,* London: Routledge and Kegan Paul, 1966.

—— *Natural Symbols*. London: Barrie and Rockliff, 1970.

—— *Implicit Meanings*. London: Routledge and Kegan Paul, 1975.

Edel, Leon. *Henry James*. Vols. 1–5. Philadelphia: J. P. Lippincott, 1953–1972.

Edelson, Marshall. *Language and Interpretation in Psychoanalysis*. New Haven: Yale University Press, 1975.

Eissler, K. R. *Leonardo da Vinci: Psychoanalytic Notes on an Enigma*. New York: International Universities Press, 1961.

—— *Discourse on Hamlet and "Hamlet."* New York: International Universities Press, 1971.

Firth, Raymond. *Elements of Social Organization*. Boston: Beacon Press, 1963.

Fox, Robin. "Totem and Taboo Reconsidered." In Edmund Leach, ed., *The Structural Study of Myth and Totemism*. A.S.A. monograph no. 5. London: Tavistock Publications, 1967.

Freud, Sigmund. *The Standard Edition of the Complete Psychological Works of Sigmund Freud*. James Strachey, Anna Freud, Alix Strachey, and Alan Tyson, eds. London: The Hogarth Press, various dates.

—— *Gesammelte Werke*. London: Imago Publishing Company, 1942.

—— *The Origins of Psycho-Analysis: Letters to Wilhelm Fliess, Drafts and Notes 1887–1902*. Marie Bonaparte, Anna Freud, Ernst Kris, eds.; Eric Mosbacher, James Strachey, trans. New York: Basic Books, 1954.

Gay, Peter. *Art and Act: On Causes in History—Manet, Gropius, Mondrian*. New York: Harper & Row, 1976.

—— *Freud, Jews, and Other Germans*. New York: Oxford University Press, 1978.

Gill, Merton. "The Primary Process." *Psychological Issues*, nos. 2–3, monograph 18/19, 5:259–298. New York: International Universities Press, 1967.

—— *Analysis of Transference*. Vol. 1. "Theory and Technique," New York: International Universities Press, 1982.

Gombrich, Ernst. "Psycho-Analysis and the History of Art," *Meditations on a Hobby Horse*. London: Phaidon, 1963, pp. 30–44.

—— "The Use of Art for the Study of Symbols." *American Psychologist* (1965), 20:34–50.

—— "The Logic of Vanity Fair." In P. A. Schilpp, ed., *The Philosophy of Karl Popper*, 2:925–957. La Salle, Ill.: Open Court, 1974.

Graetz, H. R. *The Symbolic Language of Vincent Van Gogh*. New York: McGraw-Hill, 1963.

Greenacre, Phyllis. *Swift and Carroll*. New York: International Universities Press, 1955.

—— *Emotional Growth*. 2 vols. New York: International Universities Press, 1971, esp. chs. 18, 19 and Part II.

Grolnick, Simon A. and Leonard Barkin, eds. *Between Reality and Fantasy: Transitional Objects and Phenomena*. New York: Jason Aronson, 1978.

Habermas, Jürgen. *Knowledge and Human Interest*. Boston: Beacon Press, 1971, esp. chs. 10, 11, 12.

—— "On Systematically Distorted Communications." *Inquiry* (1970), vol. 13.

Hampshire, Stuart. *Freedom of Mind*. Princeton: Princeton University Press, 1971.

Hartmann, Heinz. *Ego Psychology and the Problem of Adaptation*. David Rapaport, trans. New York: International Universities Press, 1958.

Hartmann, Heinz and Ernst Kris. "The Genetic Approach in Psychoanalysis." In *The Psychoanalytic Study of the Child*. Vol. 1. New York: International Universities Press, 1946.

Hauser, Arnold. *Philosophy of Art History*. New York: Knopf, 1959.

Hegel, G. W. F. *Vorlesungen über die Ästhetik*. Vols. 12–14. *Sämtliche Werke*,

Jubiläumsausgabe. Herman Glockner, ed. Stuttgart, 1927. *Aesthetics: Lectures on Fine Art.* T. M. Knox, trans. Oxford: Clarendon Press, 1975.

Heiman, Marcel. "Psychoanalytic Observations on the Last Painting and Suicide of Vincent Van Gogh." *International Journal of Psychoanalysis* (1976) 57:71.

Henrich, Dieter. "Self-Consciousness: A Critical Introduction to a Theory." *Man and World* (1971), 4:3–28.

Hoffman, Frederick J. *Freudianism and the Literary Mind.* Baton Rouge: Louisiana State University Press, 1945.

Hofstadter, Albert and Richard Kuhns. *Philosophies of Art and Beauty.* Chicago: University of Chicago Press, 1976.

Holland, Norman N. *Psychoanalysis and Shakespeare.* New York: McGraw-Hill, 1966.

—— *The Dynamics of Literary Response.* New York: Oxford University Press, 1968.

Jakobson, Roman. *Fundamentals of Language.* The Hague: Mouton, 1956.

Jones, Ernest. *Hamlet and Oedipus.* New York: Anchor Books, 1949.

Katan, M. "A Causerie on Henry James's "The Turn of the Screw," *Psychoanalytic Study of the Child,* (1962 and 1966), vols. 17 and 21.

Kernberg, Otto. "The Dynamic Unconscious and the Self." Unpublished article.

Klein, Melanie. *New Directions in Psychoanalysis.* New York: Basic Books, 1957.

Kohut, Heinz. " 'Death in Venice' by Thomas Mann." *Psychoanalytic Quarterly* (1957), 26:206–228.

Kris, Ernst. *Psychoanalytic Explorations in Art.* New York: International Universities Press, 1952.

Kuhns, Richard. *The House, The City, and the Judge: The Growth of Moral Awareness in the Oresteia.* Indianapolis: Bobbs Merrill, 1962.

—— *Structures of Experience: Essays on the Affinity Between Philosophy and Literature.* New York: Basic Books, 1970; New York: Harper Torchbook, 1974.

—— "Deletion and Compression in Poetry." *Foundations of Language* (1974) 11:401–407.

—— "Hume's Republic and the Universe of Newton." In Peter Gay, ed., *Nineteenth-Century Studies,* pp. 73–95. Presented to Arthur M. Wilson. Hanover, N.H.: University Press of New England, 1972.

—— "Metaphor as Plausible Inference in Poetry and Philosophy." *Philosophy and Literature* (1979), 3(2):255–237.

—— "That Kant Did Not Complete His Argument Concerning the Relation of Art to Morality and How It Might Be Completed." *Idealistic Studies* (1975) (2):190–206.

—— "Philosophical Anthropology." *Social Research* (Winter 1980), 47(4):721–733.

—— "The Beautiful and the Sublime." *New Literary History* (1981–82), 13:287–307.

Lacan, Jacques. *Écrits*. Paris: Edition du Seuil, 1966.

—— "The Insistence of the Letter in the Unconscious." *Yale French Studies* (1966), 36–37:112–147.

Laplanche, J. and J.-B. Pontalis. *The Language of Psycho-Analysis*, trans. Donald Nicholson-Smith. New York: W. W. Norton, 1973.

Leach, Edmund. *Genesis as Myth and Other Essays*. London: Jonathan Cape, 1969.

Lévi-Strauss, Claude. *The Scope of Anthropology*. London: Jonathan Cape, 1967.

Liebert, Robert S. *Michelangelo: A Psychoanalytic Study of His Life and Images*. New Haven and London: Yale University Press 1983.

Mannheim, Karl. "On the Interpretation of Weltanschauung." In Paul Kecskemeti, ed., *Essays on the Sociology of Knowledge*. London: Routledge and Kegan Paul, 1952.

Marcuse, Herbert. *Eros and Civilization*. Boston: Beacon Press, 1955.

Meyer, Bernard C. *Joseph Conrad: A Psychoanalytic Biography*. Princeton: Princeton University Press, 1967.

—— "Some Reflections on the Contributions of Psychoanalysis to Biography." In Robert B. Holt and Emanuel Peterfreund, eds., *Psychoanalysis and Contemporary Science*. Vol. 1. New York: Macmillan, 1972.

Muensterberger, Warner. *Man and His Culture: Psychoanalytic Anthropology After "Totem and Taboo."* New York: Taplinger, 1970.

Murray, Henry A. "Introduction." *Pierre, or the Ambiguities,* by Herman Melville. New York: Farrar Strauss, 1949, pp. xiii–ciii.

Nietzsche, Friedrich. *The Birth of Tragedy*. Francis Gollfing, tr. New York: Anchor Books, 1956.

Nolan, Barbara. *The Gothic Visionary Perspective*. Princeton: Princeton University Press, 1977.

Orlando, Francesco. *Toward a Freudian Theory of Literature, with An Analysis of Racine's Phèdre*. Charmaine Lee, trans. Baltimore: Johns Hopkins University Press, 1978.

Painter, George. *Proust*. Boston: Little, Brown, 1959.

Phillips, William, ed. *Art and Psychoanalysis*. New York: Meridian Books, 1963.

Rank, Otto. *Das Inzest-Motiv in Dichtung und Sage: Grundzuge einer Psychologie des Dichterischen*. Vienna: Shaffens, 1912.

—— Der Doppelgänger: Eine Psychoanalytische Studie. Leipzig, Vienna, Zurich: Internationaler Psychoanalytischer Verlag, 1925. *The Double*. Harry Tucker, Jr., trans. Chapel Hill: University of North Carolina Press, 1971.

Rappaport, David. "The Conceptual Model of Psychoanalysis." In *The Collected Papers of David Rapaport*, pp. 405–431. New York: Basic Books, 1967.

Ricoeur, Paul. *De l'interpretation: essai sur Freud.* Paris: Edition du Seuil, 1965. *Freud and Philosophy: An Essay on Interpretation.* Denis Savage, trans. New Haven: Yale University Press, 1970.

Rose, Gilbert J. *The Power of Form.* New York: International Universities Press, 1980.

Rubinstein, Benjamin. "On Metaphor and Related Phenomena." In Robert B. Holt and Emanuel Peterfreund, eds., *Psychoanalysis and Contemporary Science.* Vol. 1. New York: Macmillan, 1972.

Ruitenbeek, Hendrik M., ed. *The Literary Imagination: Psychoanalysis and the Genius of the Writer.* Chicago: Quadrangle Books, 1965.

Sandler, Joseph. "On the Concept of the Superego." *Psychoanalytic Study of the Child* (1960), 15:128–162.

Sandler, Joseph and Anne-Marie Sandler. "On the Development of Object Relations and Affects." *International Journal of Psycho-Analysis* (1978), 59:285–296.

Sartre, Jean-Paul. *L'Idiot de la famille: Gustave Flaubert de 1821 à 1857.* Paris: Gallimard, 1971.

—— "Question de methode." *Critique de la raison dialectique.* Vol. 1. Paris: Gallimard, 1960.

Schafer, Roy. *Aspects of Internalization.* New York: International Universities Press, 1968.

Schapiro, Meyer. "Two Slips of Leonardo and a Slip of Freud." *Psychoanalysis* (1955–56), 2:3–8.

—— "Leonardo and Freud: An Art-Historical Study." *Journal of the History of Ideas.* (1956) 17:147–178.

—— "The Apples of Cézanne." *Art News Annual* (1968), 34:35–53.

Schur, Max. *The Id and the Regulatory Principles of Mental Functioning.* New York: International Universities Press, 1966.

Sharpe, Ella Freeman. *Collected Papers on Psychoanalysis.* London: Hogarth Press, 1950.

Shope, Robert K. "Freud's Concept of Meaning." In Benjamin R. Rubinstein, ed., *Psychoanalysis and Contemporary Science,* 2:276–303. New York: Macmillan, 1973.

Simmel, Georg. "How Is Society Possible?" In Maurice Natanson, ed., *Philosophy of the Social Sciences,* pp. 73–92. New York: Random House, 1963.

Smith, Joseph, ed. *Psychoanalysis and Language.* Vol. 3, *Psychiatry and the Humanities.* New Haven: Yale University Press, 1978.

Sommerhof, G. *Analytical Biology.* London: Oxford University Press, 1950.

Spector, Jack J. *The Aesthetics of Freud.* New York: Praeger, 1973.

—— *Delacroix: The Death of Sardanapalus.* New York: Viking Press, 1974.

Stokes, Adrian. *Three Essays on the Painting of Our Time.* London: Tavistock, 1961.

—— *The Invitation in Art.* New York: Chilmark Press, 1965.

—— *Selected Writings.* Richard Wollheim, ed. London: Penguin Books, 1972.

Winnicott, D. W. "Transitional Objects and Transitional Phenomena." *International Journal of Psycho-Analysis* (1953), 34:433–456.

—— *The Maturational Processes and the Facilitating Environment: Studies in the Theory of Emotional Development.* New York: International Universities Press, 1965.

Wolfenstein, Martha. "The Image of the Lost Parent." *Psychoanalytic Study of the Child* (New Haven: Yale University Press, 1973), 28:433–456.

Wolff, Cynthia Griffin. *A Feast of Words: The Triumph of Edith Wharton.* New York: Oxford University Press, 1977.

Wollheim, Richard. *Sigmund Freud.* New York: Viking Press, 1971.

—— *On Art and the Mind.* Cambridge, Mass.: Harvard University Press, 1974.

The following journals and serials have many useful articles on the psychoanalytic theory of art and on psychoanalytic interpretations of art.

American Imago, A Psychoanalytical Journal for the Arts and Sciences, 1939—.

Imago, Zeitschrift für Anwendung der Psychoanalyse auf die Geisteswissenschaften. Leipsig: Internationaler Psychoanalytischer Verlag, 1912–1917/19; 1921–36.

The Psychoanalytic Study of the Child.

Psychoanalysis and Contemporary Science.

Psychoanalysis and the Social Sciences.

Yale French Studies.

Index